Vito's
Journey

Vito's
Journey

VITO A. LEPORE

iUniverse, Inc.
Bloomington

Vito's Journey

iUniverse books may be ordered through booksellers or by contacting:

iUniverse
1663 Liberty Drive
Bloomington, IN 47403
www.iuniverse.com
1-800-Authors (1-800-288-4677)

ISBN: 978-1-4620-5337-7 (sc)
ISBN: 978-1-4620-5338-4 (ebk)

Printed in the United States of America

iUniverse rev. date: 09/13/2011

For my mother

TABLE OF CONTENTS

PREFACE

9/10/2002

Why? What would be the purpose of writing the memoirs of my life? I didn't attain high office, didn't invent anything revolutionary, and probably have had more failures than successes.

The fact is I believe I did make a difference, as I believe every human being makes a difference. We don't all make it into the history books, but we all touch other lives, and sometimes have an effect on those lives, sometimes for the better, and sometimes for the worse. Beyond that, each of us is a link from those before us, to those that follow. It's not a far reach to conclude that one person's life would have an effect on many generations to follow. You will see how a handful of people had a large part in the forming of my character, and I believe this happens to us all.

The big difference is there is no shortage of people who write the histories of the rich and famous, but those of more humble beginnings and accomplishments are forgotten after a few generations. By writing my story, I will be honoring the memory of those in my life, and passing on their stories, which would otherwise be forgotten.

Also, my children were always fascinated when we started telling old family stories, and were always curious about "where we came from". Nowadays, I'm surprised by how much they remember, and by how much they've forgotten.

This is a work in progress. The starting date is noted above, but I have no idea how long it will take, or if it will even be completed. I have a very rough idea of what I'd like to do, but "Fra il dire e il fare, c'e di mezzo il mare." Between saying and doing, there is the sea. You may recognize it better as "Talk is cheap". When I used to get particularly carried away with a project, my mother would smile, and with the above phrase, remind me that at some point I would have to put in some work. Although she was always supportive, we both knew work was not my strong suite.

I would like the contents to be historically correct, but also informative and entertaining. The intent is to be objective, but it is, after all, <u>. . . as I saw it !!!</u>

11/26/2010

It's the day after Thanksgiving, and a quick calculation will tell the reader that I have been at this, off and on, for a little over eight years. Since I have a better idea now than I did then, it's time for an addendum.

I thought I would have been done by now, but I'm just into the 60's, the biggest problem being deciding what to put down. This has not been due to lack of material, but rather because there was too much! I've been amazed at how many forks in the road there have been in my life, and how so many of them have dramatically affected it. If for no reason other than that, it is a worthwhile read. In doing so, I believe you will also become conscious of the forks in the road of your own life, which could be very constructive for you. Maybe the biggest lesson learned is that there is no such thing as a last chance!

So far, I'm satisfied with what I've done. I think it's informative and entertaining. I hope the reader will also find this so, as we journey through my life.

8/22/2011

Today is an historic day for me. It is the 98th anniversary of my father's landing on Ellis Island, leading to my good fortune of being born and raised in the greatest country that's ever been.

Today is also the day I am reviewing my manuscript for publication. It's yet another fork in the long road of my life, and I'm excited as to where it may lead. What started out as a memoir of family history has evolved into what I believe is an interesting story for all to enjoy. The hope is that the reader will also be induced to reflect on their own family history, and the characters therein, which could lead to some very interesting stories of their own.

Happy trails,

Vito

Family History

Sciancalepore is the original family name. Having a last name is a relatively new tradition, over the last couple thousand years. Depending on the culture, it could have originated as a reference to the clan or the feudal lord of the individual; It could be the city or town you came from; It could be a reference to your trade; It could be a nickname, or a variation of any of the above.

Apparently, Sciancalepore was a nickname. "scianca" means "to maim", and "lepore" is a variation of "lepre", or hare or wild rabbit. So, it seems an early ancestor was good at rabbit hunting. Probably had a great arm, and was a very accurate rock thrower. That could explain why, when I played baseball, I always wanted to pitch. It would also explain why I wasn't very good! My fastball was OK, but I couldn't throw a good curve ball. Of course! How many rabbits would my ancestor have hit if the rock he threw kept curving?

Anyway, "Sciancalepore" is not a very common name, but there are many with the name today in the town of Molfetta, in the province of Bari, Italy. My grandfather moved from Molfetta to Corato, which is a couple of towns away.

Cristina Sciancalepore   Vito Sciancalepore

My grandfather, Vito Sciancalepore, was a shoemaker. Had nine children, four boys, and five girls. I'm sure he had at least one brother, I think called Donato, so there may be "Sciancalepore" on that branch of the family. On our side, of the four boys, my father had two boys (myself and Mike). My uncle Larry had a boy (Vito), and a girl (Christine). Uncle Dan and uncle Ralph had no children.

I had two boys and a girl. Mike had a boy and girl. Little Vito had a girl. So, the bottom line is there were 4 boys in my father's generation, 3 boys in my generation, and three boys in the next generation. Of those, only Gregory has had any boys so far (David and Michael). Unless we have a couple of prolific generations, the family name will go the way of the Dodo bird.

As I became Americanized in the 1940's, the name Sciancalepore was a hindrance to me wherever I went. People couldn't pronounce it, couldn't spell it, and it was easy to distort it. So, I became "Singapore", "Shank", "Skank", etc. Sometime early in high school, I started using "Lepore" informally, and left "Sciancalepore" only for official records.

When I was drafted into the Army in 1952, I used the name Lepore, and it became my name for all records. I officially changed the name to Lepore in 1954: At a special term, Part II, of the City Court, of the City of New York, County of Bronx, at the courthouse, 851 Grand Concourse, on the 20th day of September, 1954. Present: Justice William S. Evans authorized the use of the name Lepore as of the 1st day of Nov. 1954.

My brother Mike, and cousin Vito, also switched to Lepore, although I don't know if they did it legally as I did. Therefore, "Sciancalepore" no longer exists in the family.

* * *

Born 10/31/1903
<u>Maria Teresa Venturina Gigerra</u>
Vernice - CORATO 1904

<u>My mother</u>—Maria Vernice Sciancalepore (1903-1958)
(Excerpt taken from my "Notes to David Lepore—for his 18th birthday") written 4/28/1998

As a general rule, my purpose is not to give you a boring set of statistics, but to introduce you to people that have been important in my life, and have helped to form my character and outlook. To let you see them as I saw them, and in that manner, to keep them alive in our memories. In order of importance, the first choice is my mother!

After telling you that I'm not going to bore you with statistics, I will start off with a statistic! My mother and I share a birth-date. We were both born on Halloween, she in 1903, and me in 1930.

She was my biggest fan; had a lot of faith in me; backed me in all aspects of my life, and took a lot of grief from my father because of me. I wish I could say I fulfilled her expectations, but it would be a lie! Where my mother is concerned, if wishes were musical instruments, I could have been a Symphony orchestra! She died on Mothers' Day 1958, much too young and much too quickly! She was diagnosed with Leukemia in January, and gone in May! Leaving me with all these years, and all these wishes. Let me tell you about her.

Whether in Italy or here, young or older, people who knew her referred to her as a "vera signora", a real lady. This meant she had a presence, a bearing, which was independent of wealth or status, which we didn't have. Of course, she raised our status, and we always knew we were special and above normal because of her. This doesn't suggest that she was stuffy! She had a great sense of humor, and wasn't afraid to try new things. She was almost fifty years old when she decided to learn to drive, and got a driver's license, and the first family car. When my teen age brother Mike got a convertible, he made her put on his leather jacket, his long scarf (like a World War I aviator), pinned back her hair, and asked her to drive the car. I still remember her, taking off alone, scarf flying and double exhaust rumbling to wake the neighborhood, and enjoying the new experience.

When she met my mother-in-law-to-be in Italy, they got along great, even though my mother-in-law was more "earthy", and told dirty jokes. She enjoyed it, and held her own, but never ever lost her sense of dignity and propriety, even to the end.

When she left the house for the last time, to go to the hospital, she was too weak to go down the stairs by herself. So, we sat her on the kitchen chair, and my brother and I carried her downstairs. Even so, she told me she didn't want to make a scene, and be seen that way by the neighbors. So, when we got to the bottom of the stairs, my brother and I held her up between us, and she walked to the car.

I don't ever remember her shouting or losing her temper. "Upset" was as far as she would go, although I was capable of getting her to be "extremely upset".

I always awoke to her singing in the kitchen. It could be a ditty or an operatic aria, or just humming, but I knew she was there, and that I should start my day. However, she had this thing about "airing out" the apartment, and would open all the windows each morning, regardless of the weather. It was OK in the summer, but in the winter? I made sure I got up and dressed warm before she did her thing. Sometimes, I didn't make it, like on weekends. To be caught in your underwear in the middle of winter is no fun!

She was born in Corato (Bari), was the first-born, followed by two brothers and a sister: Gennaro, Esterina, and Amerigo, in that order. Her parents were Michele and Teresa, and there's a story there!

Michele Vernice (5/8/1870-2/14/1961)
Teresa Antro Vernice (1872-1947)

Briefly, my grandmother's maiden name was Antro, from a very well-to-do family from the town of Giovinazzo (about 25-30 miles away). My grandfather was a building contractor, and was doing work at the Antro villa. They met and fell in love. One thing led to another, and she ran away with him to get married, because her family would never have approved. In those days, if a girl took off with a boy without permission, she became instantly "soiled", and better marry that boy! Her family disowned her! Occasionally, her two aunts would come to visit her on the sneak, but that was it!

1920's
Maria and Aunt—Antro

I was in Italy until I was nine years old, and I remember her. A rather delicate woman, very kind, very soft-spoken. One of my chores was to occasionally go and make frequent trips to the public fountain, and fill my grandparents' large clay containers (like in "Ali Baba and the Forty Thieves") with water. Although it was common to speak dialect, my grandmother preferred to speak true Italian, and would tolerate no nonsense.

Esterina - Teresa Antro Vernice
Tedeschi - Vito and Isa - 1941

Esterina Vernice Tedeschi (8/16/1905-12/6/1948)

As I said before, my grandfather was a building contractor, apparently not overly successful (my mother once told me that he had more cases in court than he had jobs to do). He always commanded respect! When I last saw him in the 1950's, he was in his 80's, and living with his married son Amerigo (my favorite relative). He still maintained his schedule of going to his studio office every day, and buying a little something on his way home for dinner. Sometimes ricotta, cold cuts, bread, etc. I suppose it was his way of not feeling beholden for his care by his children. What struck me was that, even then, no one would sit at the dinner table until he came home, and when he did, my grandfather was the last to sit down! He had medical problems, but he handled them privately, and never made a fuss about himself. He had a very strong personality. My mother recalled seeing him sitting on his balcony, watching people passing by, while a doctor proceeded to lance his forearm on four sides, and then swab the open wounds to cleanse the infection!

When I was little, I remember spending many days with him while he was doing work at Corato's cemetery. He didn't do a lot of talking, but was very caring. He always carried some candy in his pockets for me, and I enjoyed going back and forth, being given a ride on his bicycle.

As for my grandmother, besides the aunts' occasional visits, I don't remember her having many friends. She was obviously different from the other women, like a fish out of water. However, I never heard a peep of complaint from her to anyone!

My mother once took me to Giovinazzo to see the villa her mother had grown up in. We didn't get beyond the gates, because no one was home. What I remember is the villa in the distance, and some "humongous" sunflowers by the gate! Of course, as I was seven or eight years old, the villa may have seemed further than it was, and the sunflowers larger than they were. No matter, it was still a tremendous contrast to the way my grandparents were living then! To grow up with servants and carriages, and end up without water! WOW! Now I understand that these are material things. There was a lot of genuine love and caring between my mother and the rest of her family, which no amount of money can buy.

This is where my mother came from. She had some schooling, but it wasn't much beyond grammar school. In those days, the woman's primary function was to prepare to be a wife. Unfortunately, how well you married wasn't so much dependent on your education or looks, as it was on a woman's dowry! The bigger the dowry, the better the marriage.

Corato has a circular main street, called the "Stradone" (big street). It was where the town converged. People would walk the Stradone every evening. Some would go clockwise, others counter-clockwise. When you had seen everyone going in one direction, you would reverse and see the other half, stopping occasionally for conversation, and sometimes sit at an outdoor café to have some coffee or gelato (ice cream). This was definitely a treat, not for every day!

Marriageable girls were showcased in this fashion, although in a town of 30,000, everyone already knew everyone, and dating did not exist! My mother told me that when the family walked the Stradone, her father sometimes would walk with his left hand holding his jacket lapel, with the large house-key hanging from his pinky finger. This was to tell the world that his daughters were good "home" girls. He must have been a hardheaded negotiator, because he lost a couple of wedding proposals for not providing an adequate dowry. My mother was heartbroken at missing out on someone she was particularly attracted to.

My grandfather agreed to a wedding proposal for my aunt Esterina, because he wasn't forced to provide a large dowry. Reason was that the husband-to-be didn't plan on living in Corato, so he didn't have to "save face". You see, a dowry was made public, and then, in a small town, the people would forever talk about who got the better of the deal, even years after the marriage.

My aunt Esterina couldn't have gotten married without my mother's permission. Reasons being that the older girls have to marry before the younger ones. Otherwise, it's like the kiss of death, the older one becoming less "marriageable". My mother loved her sister, and wanted her to be happy, and said OK, regardless of how it would affect her prospects

Enter my father, Ignazio Sciancalepore! Born in Corato (12/24/1894), the second boy of nine children (four boys and five girls). My grandfather Vito was a shoemaker from Molfetta, who came, and stayed in Corato, married to Christina Fascilla.

My father realized early on that things were going to be tough for him. Traditionally, the first boy gets preferential treatment, theory being he would be the first to help the family back. The other boys go out to be apprentices, at no pay, to learn a trade. My father and uncle Donato went into construction, and uncle Lorenzo, the baby, went to apprentice on making wagon-wheels. The oldest brother, Raffaele, stayed with his father, and became a shoemaker. Faced with this situation, while still a teenager, my father borrowed money from the town barber, (no signatures—only on the honor of the family name) and immigrated to America. All by himself, and armed only with a willingness to work. More on my father when I get to write about him.

Almost twenty years later he returned to Corato to find a wife. It's easy to see what he saw in my mother. On the other hand, my grandfather saw a great opportunity! Although my father was a bricklayer in America, in Corato he was "l'Americano", and presumed to be rich. Truth to tell, a bricklayer's wages in dollars in New York, became a small fortune in Lira in Corato. So, my grandfather gave a choice piece of property in the center of town as part of my mother's dowry. He then proceeded to convince my father to construct a building on the site, with him as contractor, of course!

Maria and Ignazio—1929

For years, my father complained about how my grandfather "stole" money from him, sending a stream of bills from Italy to America, to pay for the construction. My father paid, of course, but I don't think my grandfather "stole" anything, beyond his normal profit. My grandfather was an honorable man, but it was a new experience for my father, owning a building!

Via Duomo Corato - 1930's

My mother never really liked life in America, and missed her family. So, after I was born, we returned to Italy in 1932, where we stayed until just before World War II. My father went back and forth, staying long enough to help make a couple of brothers for me, and then return to New York to earn some more dollars. My mother liked and respected my father's work ethic, but they didn't have a whole lot in common. She always strived to be better, and to make the most of one-self, whereas my father saw everything in dollars and cents. Given what he had gone through, it was understandable. My father would have been happy to have me become a bricklayer, and for us to have gone to work together. However, he deferred to my mother's judgement, figuring she knew better. Now, had her first first-born lived up to her expectations, her life would have been good. The fact was she loved me, encouraged me, and backed me. Then she would catch grief from my father because of me! I never measured up to my potential, at least in her lifetime, as you will see.

Fortunately, my mother saw the war coming, and we returned to New York in 1940. My father always provided, working regardless of circumstances. My mother cared for us, and provided a haven for us to live in. We lacked for nothing, even though we didn't originally have a car, TV, etc. You see, it's a matter of perception! We didn't have any more or less than others in the neighborhood, but I just felt that if we really wanted something, we would get it. That's on the material side. On the personal side, home life was peaceful, except for the trouble I made. It was an atmosphere my mother created, which was different from others. Different from my uncle Larry, although we shared his house (separate apartments), different from any of my friends or any other people I knew. Different, but much better, at least in my mind. That's why I always felt I was better than others. I still do!

After World War II, my parents realized they weren't making any money from their building in Corato, so in 1950 my father sent my mother to Italy to see if anything could be done. My mother took my brother and myself along with her. My brother because he was little (12 years old), and me I think, to try and keep me from being drafted for the Korean War, which was breaking out.

In retrospect, this was one of those forks in the road of life, which had a tremendous effect on us. It certainly changed the course of our lives! Briefly: Because of the laws in effect in Italy at the time, the accumulated rents (less expenses) from four apartments plus two stores for eleven years was just enough to pay the rent for one month's stay in an apartment in Trani (a seashore town 8 miles away). Inflation had brought the Lira from 10/dollar in 1939 to 600/dollar in 1950. Rents couldn't be raised, and tenants couldn't be evicted! The only choice was to sell the apartments and stores at the best possible price, which my mother proceeded to do. The tenants bought the properties, and then she took a huge gamble!

I know my father would have wanted the money from the apartments brought to The States, where he could then buy a house of his own, rather than pay rent for an apartment in uncle Larry's house. I also know my mother wouldn't have done anything with the money without my father's knowledge and consent. They didn't share their business with me, so I can only guess at the motivation. I know my mother would rather live in Italy. My father also, if he could afford it. I know there was concern for me being drafted for the Korean War. I have a feeling that, since my mother's dowry was part of the value of the building, she may have felt more possessive than if it had been totally my father's. I have nothing to back this opinion up with, except that I'm sure my father had to be convinced to take this course of action. What course? To invest the money in a business!

We formed a partnership with Gino Povia, a master pastry-man in Corato. We then opened a café and pastry shop in Trani, called "Povia", with capabilities to cater weddings and other banquets. It was top-of-the-line, and drew raves for quality. It also provided a future for me, as well as a good job for my uncle Amerigo (my favorite relative), who was then earning a meager living as a chauffeur! In one fell swoop, my mother had solved all the problems, and assured all our futures! So it seemed, but it started to unravel almost at once.

Povia was a great pastry chef, but not a great business-man. He was more interested in making more of a name for himself than to make a profit. Originally, being a new business, this was justified, but was not adjusted with time. Also, my uncle Amerigo's salary was paid from our share of the profits, because he was basically there to look out for our interests. So, although the bar and catering was profitable, it wasn't returning any money for my parents' investment. Finally, in 1952, I had to return to the U.S.. The F.B.I. was becoming more insistent about my reporting for military duty. As a matter of fact, I had to report to the F.B.I. the day after I arrived in America, was slapped with an immediate induction, and was in the Army in two weeks!

Since this is about my mother, I'll skip the details of the business and my life for the next few years, except to say that by 1956 my parents hadn't received one penny back from their investment. Although I returned to Italy with my new bride in 1956, to try to salvage a bad deal, by 1957 it was a total disaster. I leave the details for another time, because they're not as important as the result!

As I said at the beginning, my mother was diagnosed with leukemia in January '58, and died in May '58. We returned to the U.S. at the end of '57, so we passed the holidays happily before the bad news. That's the medical explanation. My personal belief is different! From 1950 to 1957, I had only been living at home for about 1½ years, so my belief isn't based on actual observation. However, I know the routine as if I'd been there! After work, my father, mother, and brother would sit down for dinner. After dinner, either my uncle Larry would come up to play cards ("La scopa" or "Briscola"), or he would play cards with my mother. Nickel a game, just to play for something. Most of the time, my father enjoyed giving the "needle" to my uncle for almost anything, and it was fun. However, there were many times when he carried on about all the years that he had worked with nothing to show for it. All the money lost in the "Bar Povia". He would complain to anyone who would listen. He was innocent, but whose fault was it? Why, the person who's idea it was, aided by her useless son! Now, imagine this woman being subjected to these recriminations, almost on a daily basis, for seven years! That's a lot of grief to take! In all of that time, I never heard of her answering back, nor did she criticize me or ask more of me, for my handling of the business.

The kind of grief I'm talking about here has an expression in Italian called, "cattivo sangue" or "bad blood". I believe the continued feelings of guilt, with no outlet, always keeping it in, led to the deficient blood supply "cattivo sangue", which led to the leukemia.

She is buried in St. Raymond's Cemetery, in the Bronx, and shares a plot with my uncle Ralph and uncle Larry's brother-in-law Phil.

After she died, my brother Mike did not return to N.Y.U., where he was in pre-med, and getting good grades. He went to work with my father as a bricklayer, and later did some work on his own. His life certainly took a different path with her death. Immediate impact! Left without a rudder!

In no way am I blaming my father. As I've said somewhere else, "all is perception". My father saw life differently, based on his makeup. Also, I can't do justice to my mother in a few pages. This is just an introduction, and we'll run into her again as I recount my story . . . as I saw it.

Quite a woman! I miss her every day of my life!!!

PS—It always bothered me that my mother was buried in the ground, between two strangers. Although the headstone had only her name on it, the plot belonged to uncle Larry. Uncle Ralph had been buried there before her, and aunt Clara's brother Phil was buried there later. The plot allowed for four bodies to be stacked on top of each other. Bothered me, but never able to do something about it until exactly 43 years later. On May 8th, 2001, I arranged to have my mother's body exhumed, and join my father at an above ground mausoleum at Woodlawn Cemetery. Mike came up from Florida, shared in the expense, and we both helped her relocate. Too little, too late, but at least it's something.

*   *   *

My father—Ignazio Sciancalepore (1894-1981)
(Excerpt taken from my "Notes to David Lepore—for his 18th birthday")
Written 4/21/1999

I came very late to appreciate my father. The older I get, the more I realize how much my father accomplished, to the point that I now see him in heroic proportions.

This obviously requires some explanation, since my father was not Superman, nor did he make the front page of the news, nor was he a leader of men. He was just a hard working man; with a couple of years of schooling so he could read and write; with a supreme confidence in himself as a working man which allowed him to make some very radical decisions. Among the immigrants, there were thousands of people like my father, from different countries. Just as today, there are similar stories among the Asian and Spanish-speaking immigrants. As you read this, you may be experiencing still another wave of immigrants from another part of the world with similar courage. The great number of these people doesn't take away from their heroic exploits. It just says there are heroes all around us at all times, and that my father was one of them.

I can see the funny look on your face, asking "What's a hero?" Well, I'll briefly tell my father's story, and then you decide if it fits your definition of "hero".

He was born on December 24th, 1894, although he celebrated his birthday in January. This was common in those days, because although born earlier, they used the date they were officially registered at the town hall (Municipio). He was the second-oldest boy of nine children (4 boys and 5 girls). His father Vito was a shoemaker, and provided adequate clothing, food, and shelter for the family. It was clear though, that the children had to learn to fend for themselves as soon as possible, especially the boys! One exception! The oldest brother Ralph would follow in his father's footsteps, and take over the shop eventually. So, somewhere between the ages of nine and eleven, the boys were sent out to apprentice (at almost no pay) to learn a trade. No more school. My father and the next oldest Donato went to apprentice in construction. The youngest, Lorenzo, would go to making wagon wheels. The workday lasted from sunup to sundown, and travel to and from work was always in the dark. One of the earliest jobs my father had was working repairing an aqueduct, where he was the water boy. The horse drawn wagon would pick up the workers about 4:00AM and get to the job about 6:00AM. They would go inside these large tunnels, to replace and repair the blocks of the walls. Working in semi-darkness with lantern-light, and standing ankle deep in water, my father and his pail of water would spend the day going up and down the tunnel. Then, back on the wagon, to be home by 9:00PM, a quick meal, and to bed. Six days a week, for about one year! He received his working papers on 12/31/1905, when he was eleven years old. He kept and treasured the certificate for his whole life.

By his middle teens, he had worked his way up to be a full "muratore" (wall builder). The building blocks of the time were "tufi", or large limestone blocks. This was heavy stuff, heavy work, with little pay. Still, enough money to help with the family finances, and some left over for him. Donato wasn't doing as well, and Lorenzo was still too young, so my father was the main financial help to the family. This was not altogether a good thing, because my father could not spend his money in a way that would embarrass his older brother Ralph. Ralph, working at the family trade, didn't have the extra money my father did. So, if my father wanted to buy himself a new hat, he would have to buy one also for Ralph. The same applied for clothing and other things. Also, Ralph was not as ambitious as my father.

It became clear to my father that he was in a no-win situation, and had to find a way to earn more money. So, when he heard of this new country "America", and the possibility to earn more money, he made his break! Borrowed the trip money from the town barber (only on his word), and left for America all by himself. Ellis Island records show he arrived in New York on the ship Italia on August 22nd, 1913. He was not yet 18 years old!

Landing in New York, alone, with no money to speak of, not knowing the language—armed only with a tag hanging from his jacket had the name and address of someone from Corato that had also come to "America". Showing this tag, he eventually was directed to this person's apartment in lower New York, a section known as "Hell's Kitchen". This person welcomed him to New York, and said he could stay <u>overnight</u>!

Armed only with a willingness to work, the next morning he attacked New York! Wandering around the New York waterfront, he would approach groups of people until he found some Italians. From there, he would get leads for work, and would go anywhere and do anything honorable for a day's pay. He didn't know the language, but he got to know all the train and bus routes, so that he could get anywhere! He slept anywhere he could, and did a variety of jobs. Within a couple of years, he had made his way into the bricklayers' union, earning good money, and sending some of it home to support the family.

My father is second from the left, working as a pick and shovel man in Syracuse, N.Y. To his left is Luigi Abbattista, who he arranged to marry one of his sisters.

If you've gotten the picture that his whole existence revolved around money, then I'm telling it right! It was a trait my father kept for the rest of his life. He wasn't a cheapskate—it was just that he always compared how much work he had to do to earn the money being spent! That's why he did what he did in 1918!

World War I had broken out in Europe, and he was safe over here. However, Italian agents in New York were contacting the expatriates, trying to get them to volunteer to join the Italian army. They offered a free trip to Italy, a month's vacation at home before starting military duty, and a free trip back to New York after the war. It was a bargain my father couldn't resist! So, in a couple of months, in exchange for this great deal, he found himself on the front lines with the Italian infantry on the Austrian front. He saw death up close and personal, and was very lucky to make it out alive and unharmed. He admitted to being very very scared, but he didn't run! He saw it through! <u>Sixty years later</u>, the Italian government thanked him with a certificate as "Cavaliere", a medal, and $100 a year pension!!!

Back in New York after the war, he brought all his brothers over, and contributed money to the family, and to the sisters' dowrys, so that they married properly. He even arranged for one of the sisters to marry someone from Corato who was in America, Luigi Abbattista, from Syracuse, N.Y.

Ignazio Sciancalepore - 1924

Earning good wages, and with the building business being seasonal, allowed him to go to Corato on vacation every couple of years. There, he was "l'Americano", and a big deal in his circle of acquaintances. By 1930, at age thirty-six, he could afford to get married. I covered the details of the marriage in the notes about my mother, so we'll move on.

He brought his wife to America, where I was born on Halloween of 1930 (no laughing allowed). In 1932 we went back to Corato, to live in the building my grandfather had built, with my father's money, on my mother's property (her dowry). A brother, Michele, joined me, and my father returned to the U.S. to work. Until 1939, he made a couple of trips back and forth, my brother died of pneumonia (which he caught from my cold), and another brother also named Michele was born in 1938. My father would have liked to stay, but he couldn't afford it. He opened a store, selling goods for the home, like wax paper, kerosene for lamps, olive oil, and odds and ends, but it was a no-go. I was old enough to mind the store to give him a hand, but even at that age I wondered why anyone would come in: No electric lights, so it was dark; no big selection of merchandise, and of the little there was, it was sold for pennies. It was certainly not enough to support a family. In the few times I was there, I remember only two customers (one for kerosene, and one for a couple of sheets of wax paper). I understand he had some legitimate offers to go into a couple of partnerships, but it wasn't his cup of tea, and he didn't want to take chances with his hard-earned money. It was just as well, for war had broken out in Europe, and it was a dangerous place to be, with Mussolini in charge of Italy. In 1940, my mother, brother and I, rejoined my father in the U.S., just before the U.S. got into World War II.

I'd like to note, again, that my father was a willing worker. In the '30's, during our great depression with high unemployment, my father always worked. During World War II, there was little new construction, but my father worked. He went to the Bethlehem Shipyard, and worked as a tinsmith. How he managed that, I don't know. After the war, there was a building boom, and master bricklayers were in great demand. Construction foremen would come in their cars to pick up my father from the house, and bring him to the construction site. He was the first to be hired, and the last to be let go when the building was finished. Often he was kept on, at regular pay, doing almost nothing, until the next building was ready to go. Not only was he earning high union wages, but was also getting an extra $50-100 a week off the books to keep him happy! Let me explain briefly why a master bricklayer was so important to a builder.

A brick building goes up corner-first. That is, first you build the corners, and then you fill in the wall. The two sides, as well as the edge, had to go up straight. My father could look at a finished building, and point out where the work was second-grade. To you and I, it wouldn't mean anything, but if you or I were a builder, it would mean a great deal. Furthermore, the corner-men controlled the tempo of the work, much like coxswains in a regatta, or the drumbeater on the old sailing ships! This was because a line was pulled tight from corner to corner, so that the layer of bricks on the in-between wall would be level and uniform. A good corner-man, from the company's point of view, would try to get the bricklayers on the wall to work faster, sometimes moving the line up to the next level before all the bricklayers had finished their section. This showed up the bricklayers that weren't so fast, and if the foreman happened to see it, the guy may not be hired for the next job. A corner-man might also taunt the slower linemen, to get them to work harder. Like some chefs, corner-men could be very temperamental! Pity the poor laborer who mixed a batch of mortar that was too soft or too hard, or didn't stack a supply of bricks quickly enough, or handy enough. The whole thing could be thrown down on him from the scaffold, or the laborer could be fired. Some exceptional corner-men had their preferred laborers, like a knight had his lackey.

Make no mistake, on a job site, there was a definite caste system, and the corner-man was high-class. He could mean getting a building built faster, with more profits for the builder. Needless to say, my father wasn't very popular among the bricklayers, but he missed very few paychecks, and he worked very hard! He would say, "I work for the people who put the bread on my table." If the weather conditions weren't right, there would be no work. No work, no pay! I remember being awakened at 4-5 o'clock in the morning, as my father crossed my bedroom in his one-piece flannel underwear (with the trap-door in the back), to go to the window to check the outside thermometer, to see if it was too cold to go to work. If it was too cold to mix mortar, then no work. No matter, even if it was too cold, he would still go to the job, on the off chance he could put in a day's work doing something.

He always provided, and we never wanted for anything! No credit—everything was cash! Not even a checking account! When my mother convinced him to buy a car, he bought a brand-new '53 Mercury, all cash!

How was he as a person? When I was little, I remember following him when we went for walks. He always walked a little fast, and with a certain swagger. In Corato, he enjoyed being "L'Americano". He liked to "needle" people, (making fun), and was generally in good humor. He would tend to get down if he wasn't working, or had no prospect of a job, or when he reviewed what was being spent to keep the family going.

Of course, there was also me! I always upset him! I was always late for dinner because I was playing ball. Sweating and working hard, and <u>not earning money</u>, just did not compute! At my age, he was supporting a family, while I had a nice allowance, went to private school, got new clothes before I outgrew the old ones, and played ball! I was the first-born; he loved me, and was impatient to see me fulfill his dreams. It took a while, but he eventually became proud of me.

He would have liked to have his own house here in America, but couldn't put enough cash aside to do it. In 1944, uncle Larry bought a house on 243rd Street in the Bronx, on the Mt. Vernon border. He turned it into a two-family Home, and we rented there until both my mother and father passed away. My father and uncle would get together every night after dinner, and play cards for pennies. My uncle Larry was the perfect foil for my father. He was easy-going, and my father picked on him for laughs all the time, and uncle Larry would go along and laugh too. He was no dope, but just sure of himself, and enjoyed spending time with his big brother.

My father always behaved as if <u>he</u> owned the house, and uncle Larry was the tenant, and that was OK. Where my father had always worked for someone, my uncle had always been on his own. He had been an iceman in Harlem for many years. Before refrigerators, he would carry a 10-cent piece of ice up six floors (no elevators) for the iceboxes in the apartments. A 25-cent order was a big deal! He did this for many years and earned very good money. When he got too old for the ice business, he opened up a bar in the Bronx, a tougher place than Harlem (an area off Simpson Street known as "Fort Apache"—there was a movie made of the area by that name starring Paul Newman). He carried along with him, as a partner, his older brother Donato, who wouldn't have made it on his own. He also set up his oldest brother Ralph with his own shoemaker shop twice, but it didn't work out. Uncle Ralph didn't have the drive, and he liked to drink more than work.

When I came back from Italy in 1957, broke, married, and with one child, uncle Larry gave me a job and a very good salary, to manage his bar on weekends. That way I was able to attend classes at NYU during the week. After a couple of years I was overwhelmed by the job and had to quit. I didn't have his guts in that atmosphere, where drugs and fights were part of the nightly routine.

Later on, he borrowed money from the bank, and gave it to me, so that my brother and I could buy our own business (a newspaper route on Long Island). When we paid him back a couple of years later, we wanted to give him a large bonus, but he wouldn't take it. All he wanted was the interest he had to pay to the bank. Also, he asked us to remember, and to keep an eye on his family in the future, in case they may need help. In his broken English, he would say, "If you want to, you do!" It certainly was a great motto to live by.

After my mother passed on in '58, my father managed for awhile, and in '60 went back to Italy shopping for a new wife. In spite of being 66 years old, he was still "L'Americano" and things don't change quickly in backward small towns in Southern Italy. So, he made himself available, and once again came up with a winner. Vincenza LaFortezza was an educated and handsome woman, who had spent her life caring for her sister's children, and then her old aunt. I believe there had been a lost love of which she had never gotten over, but we never spoke of these things, so I don't know for sure. She was a great cook, didn't drink or smoke, had a very happy personality, and she was 42 years old! What a deal! Furthermore, in the 20-odd years they were married, she plainly showed she cared for him, and always respected him, and remembered him fondly after he died.

So, my father's latter years became his reward for his life of hard work. A young happy wife, cooked meals twice a day, his brother to pick on every night! A great life! Plus, with my brother and me out of the house, he was saving more money in his sixties than he ever had in his life before!

He retired in his early 70's, we saw each other regularly, and he was happy. Always healthy and with a good appetite, his main enjoyment was eating, picking on his brother, seeing us regularly, and watching wrestling on TV. Especially wrestling! He would sit on the edge of the chair, and twist and turn with the wrestlers, and curse at the bad guy, and cheer when the good guy would win, especially if he had an Italian name. Antonino Rocco was a God!

He would start shopping in August for Christmas toys for the grandchildren, and always came up with good ones, but the best one was the surrey, which my kids rode to death.

If there was one thing that bothered him more than the rest, it was money! Surprise, surprise! He would get upset if he spent the pension money, the social security money, or the interest on his savings, and had to touch his actual savings! So, my brother and I started paying the rent, bought him a bigger new TV, a washing machine, a couple of trips upstate, and he was OK. Of course, there were times when he didn't like to see me coming, because I would be taking him to the dentist to have a tooth pulled, or to a doctor for shots, but generally life was what he wanted, and pain-free.

He was in his mid-eighties when he died on July 11, 1981. After a good lunch, he stretched out in his Lazy-boy chair for his afternoon nap. From nap to coma, he never awoke. No pain, no fuss. A fitting ending for a life of hard work, I think.

There are so many other memories that come to mind; I know I'm not doing him justice in these few pages. We'll come across him in future stories, but there's one I have to share with you now.

One day, my mother turned to my father and said, "Ignazio, every day you come from work, you get off the train, and on the way home you pass all the stores. Why don't you stop by one of them, buy something, and bring it home and surprise me?" My father, puzzled, asked "Like what?"

My mother, in an exasperated tone, replied, "It doesn't matter! It's just to do something different. You could even buy radishes!" My father, still puzzled, nodded and went about his business. The next day, when he came home from work, he called out, "Maria, see what I brought you?" It was a bunch of radishes! My mother put on a happy face, and said, "Bravo Ignazio." At least, it was a start! The next day, when he came home again, again he called out, and again another bunch of radishes! When he did it again for the 3ʳᵈ day in a row, my mother realized he hadn't gotten the message, and said, "Ignazio, please, no more radishes!" He said OK, and brought nothing thereafter.

Having missed out on my young years, he tried to enjoy my brother's, who is eight years younger than I. After dinner, after a long day's work, he would sometimes try to tell him a story. He would sit Mike on his lap, on the sofa, and would start the story, "Once upon a time, there was a little doggie. The little doggie was walking along, and sometimes he would bark." We never found out what else this dog did, because about this time my father would fall asleep!

A hard worker, a good man, who made it possible for his siblings to have a better life, and who made it possible for my brother and I to raise ourselves up to the next level. My definition of a hero!

*   *   *

Family Stories

The "Mikey" stories:

These are my favorites. They are about my brother Mike. He was a lovable kid, but things seemed to happen to him that were very funny, although he didn't mean it to be that way.

The Paper Bag—

After we lost our mother to leukemia on Mother's Day 1958, my brother, without our mother's support, dropped out of school at NYU, where he was a pre-medical student. Short of cash, and twenty years old, he decided to go into business for himself. Having worked with our father as a bricklayer and helper, home repairs seemed a natural way to go. He got jobs, but it was tough going, and cash was still elusive. Long hours of work, plus extra hours to go around to collect for work already done. This is the background for the story.

At the end of a long day's work, Mike was heading home in his pick-up truck. He was tired and cold, made worse because the truck windows wouldn't close. All of a sudden, he had a bright idea! Reaching over the seat, he took a large paper bag used to carry his lunch, tore a couple of holes to see through, and slipped it over his head. Much better! His breath warmed his face, and he was more comfortable.

Unfortunately, he had not made a hole for his mouth, so he was breathing mostly recycled air. This contributed to his becoming a bit drowsy, and his reflexes were not what they should have been. So, when he approached an intersection, and the traffic light changed to red, he did not brake as quickly as he should have. The car in front had already come to a full stop when Mike bumped into his rear.

At this point, two reactions happened at the same time. The guy that was hit jumped out of his car, very indignant, to confront the person who had rammed him; Mike was jolted awake, saw what had just happened, jumped out of the truck, and ran towards the other driver, concerned to see if anyone had gotten hurt. Unfortunately, he had forgotten to remove the paper bag from his head.

The driver of the car that was hit stopped in his tracks! He sees this person with a paper bag for a head, running towards him yelling, "What's the matter? What's the matter?" What would you do?

He said, "Nothing! Nothing! Everything's OK!" After which, he jumped back into his car, puts it in gear, and runs through the red light!

Just imagine the sight of this befuddled guy, standing in the middle of the street, with a paper bag over his head, wondering what just happened, while at the same time another guy is racing away from the scare of his life!

*　　*　　*

The Overheated Radiator—

In the same time period, I was with Mike, keeping him company, while he was going to collect money for work already done. The day was sunny and pleasant, and we were traveling in his pick-up truck, when the water temperature gauge started going up, and vapor began to escape from the radiator. We were traveling on the Bronx River Parkway in Westchester County, and Mike promptly pulled the truck over on the grassy shoulder, stopped, and waited for the engine to cool down. It was clear though, that we had lost too much water, and there were no stations nearby.

Running along the Parkway was a narrow stream, which gave the road its name. Mike was struck with a simple solution to the problem! He retrieved a bucket that he had in the back of the truck, made his way down the grassy slope to the edge of the stream, scooped a bucketful of water, and made his way back up to the truck to fill the radiator. When he got there, he was very surprised to find there was no water in the bucket!

On inspection, he found the bucket to have a leaky bottom! No problem! Back down the grassy slope, scoop another bucketful of water, and return to the truck, except this time hurrying up on the return! He was a little more successful this time, getting almost a cupful of water into the radiator!

Undaunted, our hero returned down the slope, repeated the procedure, and tried to return at an even faster pace!

Now, if he had moved his path over a bit with each trip, he would have had better luck! As it was, he went back and forth on the original path, and the water leaking from the bucket made the wet grass slippery and hard to get a good foothold, especially on the return trip uphill!

On his fourth trip, Mike wanted to get an especially fast start on his return! However, when he pushed off with his right foot, the wet grass made him slip, and he fell back into the stream!

Did this discourage our hero? Not on your life! Seeing as how he was already all wet from head to toe, he saw a way to get more water up to the truck! So, standing knee deep in water, he pressed the leaky bottom of the bucket against his belly. Then he squatted down so as to fill the bucket with water. From there he proceeded to climb unto the bank, and waddled back up the same path as before, which by now was really mish-mosh. Slipping and sliding all the way, he managed to make it back to the truck with more than half a bucket of water, which he then proceeded to pour into the thirsty radiator. He looked like a drowned mouse, and I couldn't stop laughing, but we were both surprised and shocked to hear loud clapping, and shouting, and whistling.

We then realized that, on the other side of the stream, and up on the opposite slope, there was a railroad station! A train had pulled in, but had decided to stay and enjoy the spectacle!

All the car windows were down, filled with passengers, waving and shouting congratulations to Mike. Even the two train engineers in the locomotive were not going anywhere, waving their caps at my brother, who sheepishly waved back.

It was a picture worth a thousand words!

*   *   *

To Hold or Not To Hold—

A few years have passed, and it is 1966. Mike and I have been partners for about seven years, and have been pretty successful with the newspaper routes we bought in 1959. So much so, that we decided to sell them and invest all the money in a rock and roll nightclub.

Mike is now 26 years old, and married, with children. It's too bad that he had started to lose his hair in his early 20's, and was very conscious of the loss. To compensate, he got himself fitted with a hairpiece. It looked good, and made him feel at home with the club crowd, which were mainly college kids. He was closer to their age than I was, and it worked to our advantage.

The club was very popular. The capacity was for 295, but we routinely had over 500 dancing inside, with another 200 or so waiting outside to get in, if anyone left.

Almost every night a fight would break out, so we had fifteen bouncers available to keep order. For the most part it worked pretty well, and we were making a lot of money. I supervised at the door, and Mike mingled with the crowd. One night, Mike was making his way through a very crowded dance floor, when a fight broke out right in front of him! Two really big guys! Now Mike is not really a street fighter, so he waves frantically to the bouncers for help. They responded, but the dance floor was so crowded, they had a hard time getting through.

Mike had to do something! So he decided to jump on the back of one of the big guys, wrap his arms around the guy's shoulders, and tell him to settle down.

Far from settling down, the guy is enraged by this monkey on his back, and tells Mike to get the f . . . off his back, RIGHT NOW! Of course, Mike has no choice but to hold on even tighter! This makes the situation worse, and the big man starts jumping up and down, trying to shake Mike off his back!

With every jump and hard landing, Mike feels his toupee wanting to separate from his scalp! It is glued on, but it was not intended to be subjected to such abuse!

What a dilemma! What to do? Mike had two visions—One was to hold on, and have his toupee fly off, which would have made for a hilarious scene, and from which he would become the butt of jokes forever!—The other was to let go, at which point this gorilla would turn around and beat him to a bloody pulp, and hurt him very badly in the process. What to do, what to do!

Well, discretion being the better part of valor, Mike decided to hold on! So, the people made room to watch this human broncobuster, and see how long he could hang on. Up and down, up and down, stomping and cursing, but Mike wouldn't let go!

The story has a happy ending. The bouncers did get there in time, and threw the guys out. The toupee held strong, Mike got a big applause, and became a hero and crowd favorite.

Later he told me that if he had not been so afraid, he never would have been able to hold on so tight! I tell you, he was cute!

*   *   *

Mike Lepore, a.k.a. "Short Shaft"—

We used to take frequent vacations in Lake George, and Mike really liked it there. We used to stay up the lake in Bolton Landing at a place called "The Antlers", and rented motorboats from Lamb Brothers to get around and have fun. Mike always looked forward to having a boat of his own, and was always looking in the papers for something he could afford.

He did get a good deal on a 10-15 foot boat with a trailer hitch, but without a motor. Finally, on the day before leaving for the lake, he got a deal on an outboard motor. He bought it, mounted it on the boat, hitched it to the car, loaded up the family, and left for the lake.

When he got to Lake George, he got the bright idea to surprise the guys at Lamb Brothers by pulling up to their dock in his very own boat! So he put the boat in the water at Lake George, and together with Pat and little Maria and Michael, started motoring up to Bolton Landing.

The boat was fine, the motor started up promptly, and ran smoothly. The only problem was that although the motor was at full throttle, the boat was moving very slowly and not making much headway going up the lake! So much so, that it ran out of gas!

Mike promptly hooked up the spare tank, and got underway again. Alas, the boat didn't move any faster with the second tank, than it did with the first! So, when they ran out of gas a second time, they were stuck in the middle of Lake George!

Never at a loss, Mike flagged down another boat, and hitched a ride back to town to refill his tanks, leaving Pat and the kids bobbing helplessly in the middle of Lake George.

Eventually, he got another ride back, and with refilled gas tanks, continued on his journey. However, he moved no faster than before! The motor at full throttle was pretty noisy, and Pat and the kids were beginning to get pretty nervous, especially when the gas ran out in the first tank again. Fortunately, almost at the end of the second tank of gas, they came into the dock at Lamb Brothers.

Mike made the entrance he had envisioned! He nonchalantly waved to the guys on shore, and they were duly impressed with the fact that Mike had followed up on his intention to have his very own boat, and congratulated him on his seamanship, and on how smoothly he had docked the boat.

After the backslapping and welcoming, Mike told them of how long it had taken him to get there, and asked them to take a look to see if they could figure the reason why it had taken four tanks of gas to get there!

These fellows had spent their whole lives on the lake, and around boats, and it took them every bit of ten seconds to identify the problem! The first one noticed it, started laughing, and could only wave to the others, and point to the cause of the problem. They, in turn, looked, giggled, started to laugh, and couldn't stop! Mike figured he had done it again, and felt foolish without knowing the reason why.

Eventually, things calmed down enough, and it all became clear. It seems that not all boats are created equal, and neither are the outboard motors! Some boats sit higher in the water than others, so the shaft of the motor has to be long enough so the propeller is under water, and able to drive the boat.

Apparently, Mike had gotten a boat that required a motor with a long shaft, but had gotten a motor with a short shaft instead. So, the propeller barely touched the water, and was able to drive the boat only when it rocked, or if a wave from another boat came along!

Now to you and me, that may only be funny, but to boat people, that's about the stupidest thing a person purchasing a boat and motor can do. So, Mike's story was spread around town, and for quite a while he was called "Short Shaft" in public. This was especially embarrassing to Mike, because people hearing it, and not knowing the story, would give it a sexual connotation and smirk.

*   *   *

Captain Mike—

At the turn of the 70's, we were doing very well. We had our houses, money in the bank, were driving Cadillacs, and pretty much enjoying life. Mike had just bought a new boat, a 30-foot inboard-outboard motorboat, and was looking forward to taking it up to Lake George. It was a very nice-looking boat, and Mike felt like the captain of a ship. To puff his ego up even more, Pat bought him a Captain's cap and silk scarf to wear around his neck and fluff up under his chin.

Once again up to Lake George; Once again the idea to surprise the guys at Lamb Brothers by coming into their dock with his new boat; Once again putting the boat in the water in the village, and motoring up to Bolton Landing. Except this time everything went smoothly.

With his family on board, Mike was dressed impeccably, and topped off with his Captain's cap, and silk scarf fluffed under his chin.

With supreme confidence, and a lit cigarette between his lips, he approached the dock at Lamb Brothers. He waved to them nonchalantly, and upon recognizing him, they started to whoop and holler! "Nice boat", "Atta-way", "Wow", "Welcome back", were just some of the greetings.

Distracted a bit by the homecoming, and the fact that this was the first time he was docking his new boat, Mike realized he was coming in a bit wide, and would not be able to make a perfect docking.

He could have stopped, backed up, and come back for a clean docking, but after thinking about it for a millisecond, he rejected the idea. He had been boating for a few years now, and did not want to subject himself to ridicule from the lake-guys. Besides, he was the captain of this ship, and he assessed the situation, and took immediate action!

Seeing that the boat was moving very slowly, and was very near the dock, Mike decided to make it seem he had planned it that way. Motioning to Pat to get behind the wheel, he jumped up to the front of the boat, and picked up the coiled rope used to secure the boat to the dock. He made a very impressive figure; Impeccably dressed, topped by his Captain's cap, silk scarf fluffed under his chin, and a lit cigarette between his lips.

He could have tossed the rope to one of the guys, but that would have hinted that he had miscalculated! That wouldn't do! These guys notice such things! So, rope in hand, and also to show a bit of athletic ability, Mike made the little jump from boat to dock.

Disaster! By pushing off on the boat, the space between boat and dock widened immediately, and instead of landing on the dock, Mike landed in the water!

So there he was, under water, still impeccably dressed, topped by his Captain's cap, and silk scarf fluffed under his chin, and the cigarette no longer lit but drooping from between his lips, and still holding on to the rope!

He said later that at that moment, he wished he could have stayed under water forever and never come up!

But he did come up, and you can imagine the sight, and the resulting new stories about "Short-shaft"!

*   *   *

Uncle Larry Stories:

<u>Uncle Larry shows us how to kill a chicken (late 1940's)</u>

In preparation for some holiday, uncle Larry brought home a few live chickens. It was winter, so he penned them upstairs in the attic, and proceeded to fatten them up for a couple of months. He had never done anything like it before, but he proceeded like he knew all there was to know. When my father suggested that the chickens would get fatter if uncle Larry would bring the chickens downstairs to live with him, he would just laugh an "I'll show you" laugh.

Finally, the day of reckoning came, and we all gathered downstairs in uncle Larry's kitchen to see the performance. Uncle Larry brought three chickens down from the attic, put them in one of the double-sinks, and covered them.

Being young, and impressed by how self-assured he was, I stood next to him to learn how it was done, and asked him to teach me.

He proceeded to show me that you first needed a sharp knife. Then he removed the cover from the sink, lifted one chicken out, and placed it under one arm, holding the head and neck out. He then sliced the chicken's neck, put it back in the sink, and lifted another chicken out. He repeated the procedure with the other two chickens, after which he put the cover back on the sink. He then informed us that they had to "bleed" for about twenty minutes after they died, and he made use of the time by putting a large pot of water on the gas stove. By the time the chickens would be ready, the water would be boiling, and the dead chickens would be put into the boiling water for a bit. This would make it easier to remove the feathers whole.

We were all properly impressed, and even my father, who never missed a chance to make fun at his brother's expense, was driven to total silence.

Finally, the time passed, the water was boiling, and uncle Larry proceeded as planned. Turning to me, he said, "See, now I'm going remove the cover, and I'll put one chicken at a time in the boiling water, and then take off the feathers. There's really nothing to it".

Unfortunately, when he lifted the cover, what we saw were three live blinking chickens, unable to hold their heads up because their necks had been cut in half, all covered with blood!

More unfortunately, upon seeing the light, the chickens got all excited, started flapping their wings, and all three managed to escape from the sink unto the kitchen floor.

Uncle Larry, who had been momentarily frozen in place by the unexpected sight, swung into action! Chasing the chickens (who dragged their heads), around the kitchen, blood flying all over the place, he eventually got them again in the sink. This time they were mutilated, and there was no doubt that they were dead.

There was nothing in the kitchen that wasn't splattered by chicken blood, but most of it was on uncle Larry. My father was beside himself with laughter, and it was a memory he needled his brother with for the rest of his life. However, true to his nature, uncle Larry saw the humor, and laughed right along.

* * *

"C'mere, dahly"—

When my cousin Christine was a teenager, she had a crush on a boy, a nice kid. He had come from Sicily, but spoke English well. However, his skin was a little dark, and uncle Larry told Chris he didn't want her to talk to him. Of course, you can't just turn off puppy love, and Chris would find ways to run errands and "accidentally" run into him, especially since he worked part time at the local fruit and vegetable store. One day, when she was late returning from an errand, he went out looking for her. In his slippers, flannel undershirt, and suspenders holding up his pants, he asked Mike to drive him to the store. On the way, he saw Chris standing on a corner, making conversation with the dark skinned boy. "Stop the car!" he yelled, and when Mike was slow to react, so as to give his cousin more time, he got out anyway before the car came to a complete stop.

My brother tells me it was a sight to behold! When Chris and the boy (also named Mike) saw uncle Larry coming, they both took off like they had been shot out of a cannon, but in different directions. Chris headed for home, about a block and a half away, with her father in pursuit. Of course, he couldn't run very fast in slippers, and his suspenders kept falling off his shoulders, but he shuffled as fast as he could, while at the same time putting back first one suspender, then the other. He kept calling out to her, "C'mere, dahly" meaning "Come here, darling", but of course Christine wasn't listening, she was running for her life. All she had done was speak to a boy, at noon, on a warm summer day, but it was still disobedience!

She got to the house a half a block ahead of uncle Larry, closed the outside door after her, then closed the inside door, then ran into her bedroom, locked the door, and hid in the closet. Uncle Larry came at the same speed, and like a tank, went through the outside door, the inside door, smashed the bedroom door open, pulled her out of the closet, and gave her a beating (it was OK to do that in those days).

Within a two-week period, he had enrolled her in a camp for girls run by Catholic nuns in the Pocono Mountains, and shipped her off for the summer. She was allowed to return to attend high school, but the high school was in Westchester.

The romance ended, but not without a last try. I understand the young man found out where Chris was in the mountains, and got someone to give him a ride. Since aunt Clara had been with Christine on some occasions when the young lovers had spoken, he assumed she was on his side, and called to get directions to the camp. Aunt Clara obliged, but then called the nuns to advise that he was coming, and to make sure he would not be allowed on the grounds. Poor kid, three hours up, and three hours down, and never got to see her.

There is a postscript to the story. Years later, Christine met Anoush Taheri, a student immigrant from Iraq, and they would eventually marry. In the meantime, since he didn't have an apartment, uncle Larry let him sleep upstairs in the attic. He also had an Arabic nose, which he had altered by plastic surgery, and uncle Larry paid for at least part of it. All of this was not lost on my father. He would never miss an opportunity to needle his brother, especially when they played after-dinner card games. It would go something like, "So Lorenzo, tell me again, so I can understand. You didn't like that nice Italian boy, because his skin was a shade darker. Now, you bring in the house an Arab whose skin is even darker, and you let him sleep upstairs. Then you pay to fix up his hooked nose, and you're going to pay for the wedding so he can marry your daughter. Please, Lorenzo, explain so I can understand". This was always accompanied by loud cackling. Uncle Larry knew that whatever he said would only make it worse, so he would just smile, shake his head, and say "Ignazio, deal the cards."

*   *   *

"If you wanna, . . . you do!" uncle Larry

Those few words represent my most lasting memory of my uncle, as well as a lesson for us all. It's a credo that all should believe in, regardless of age or background. Unlike all my other family stories, it's not funny! It's intended to be read, be you adult, child, or in-between. Then evaluate your own behavior, and see if you need an adjustment. Anyway, here's the story.

First, I need to define uncle Larry's character. Uncle Larry had been helping people long before I came along. He was the baby of the family, and anyone who ever knew him liked him. When I spoke to his sister Lisetta in Italy about his childhood, she couldn't talk without giggling at the recollections. When I visited him in Harlem during his iceman days, the people hanging out windows were not so much ordering pieces of ice as they were making conversations with him. It seemed everyone that passed had to waive or say a word to him. Many years later, at his bar, the relationship he had with his customers was unique. It was like each one had adopted him as an honorary family member. They were predominantly black or Hispanic, but had no problem talking to him about their personal problems, and asking his opinion, while they were sober! Even the cops from the precinct took an unusual interest in the business, far above what was expected from the few dollars' weekly payoff. They would come in on their own time, in civilian clothes, just to sit and gab with him, and make sure everything was all right. He wasn't a big talker, but a good listener, and was able to say what he wanted in a few words. It was obvious that his opinions were valued.

He had a handyman named Jocko, who did odds and ends for a few bucks, which would later be spent on booze and drugs. I was amazed at his honesty and dedication when uncle Larry wasn't around (I managed the bar on weekends for almost two years). Jocko wouldn't allow any hanky-panky, no shooting-up in the bathroom, kept out anyone who was high, and escorted out anyone who became high. He was no angel, but where uncle Larry was concerned, he was the best he could be. I just had to make sure he didn't fall too far off the wagon while on duty.

Uncle Larry always loved his family, and tried to help them out. Examples that I know of are: When his oldest brother Ralph came from Italy, he set him up with his own shoemaker shop. When Ralph started drinking, and lost the shop, uncle Larry helped him recover, and set him up with another shop. He also set up aunt Clara's brother Phil with his own ice route in Harlem, but Phil failed where uncle Larry was succeeding, and left to do less demanding work. Uncle Larry's older brother Donato wasn't the brightest bulb in the pack, so uncle Larry kept him close and protected for his whole life. He got Danny an adjoining ice route, and checked on him daily. Later, he bought an interest in a second bar, and put Danny in as manager, but that didn't go too well. Uncle Danny ended his years working as a night watchman for a lumber company. He married late in life, but bought a home one block away from us, and visited uncle Larry very often, especially when he had problems, which also seemed to be very often. He didn't have anywhere near the same relationship with his other brother, my father. Lastly, after uncle Ralph's widow's death, there was talk about his properties being divided between the surviving brothers. Uncle Larry took me aside, and made me promise that if anything came of it, I would make sure his share would go to his sisters. He also had a great sense of humor, and was able to laugh at some of his own stories, such as the ones above.

On a personal basis, uncle Larry also had a significant impact. When he saw the neighborhood on 153rd Street changing for the worst, he moved uptown to 243rd Street. He bought a two-family home, and brought us with him, thereby saving us as well. When I came back from Italy, after the Bar Centrale experience, I was married, with child, and broke. He gave me a weekly salary, just to manage his bar on weekends, so that I could attend NYU days, in pursuit of an Engineering degree. I'm sure there are other examples, but these are the ones that come to mind readily. When other family members read this, they may want to add their own stories. If so, please write them down, and send them to me.

Having properly introduced you to my uncle, I can now tell you the story. After almost a couple of years at the bar, it got to be too much for me. It was a rough place, and could be dangerous. So much so, that I began dreading the thought of the weekends, and my stomach would tie up in knots. I couldn't understand how uncle Larry had managed so many years in that atmosphere. I told uncle Larry I had to leave. He understood and wished me well.

Within a year, I realized I was going nowhere fast. Working fulltime days, and going to school nights was not working out. Not enough money, didn't see my son awake except on weekends, and a degree at least four years away. So, I started looking for ways to earn more money. The most logical way was to go into business for myself, but I had no money to invest. This was in 1960. My father was still bemoaning the money lost in Italy, and wouldn't even talk about a loan. Uncle Larry sat me down, and advised me that the best way to go was to get a route. This required the least money, and would provide a good income. It had worked for him, and he asked me to check it out. For him, it had been an iceman route in Harlem. For me, it turned out to be a newspaper delivery route on Long Island. When I found one I liked, he loaned me the $2000 required for the down payment. Since my brother had dropped out of school after my mother's death, I talked him into joining me, and we both went into business with uncle Larry's money.

We did well, and about a year later, we sat down with uncle Larry to give him back his money. We wanted to give him an equal share of what we had earned, but he would have none of that! He said all he wanted, in addition to the $2000, was what he had to pay to the bank. It was only then that we found out he had borrowed the money he had lent us! All he asked, in addition, was to remember what he had done for us, in case his children ever needed help in the future.

We continued to do well, and a couple of years later, uncle Larry approached me during one of my visits to the Bronx. He said he was temporarily short of cash, and had some bills to pay. He didn't want to go to the bank, and asked me to give him some money. I honestly don't remember how much he asked for. Reason being, I was surprised by the request, and my mind was racing. Sure, we were doing OK, but we had big payments and little cash. I couldn't lay my hands on that much money right away, and I wasn't sure I could. I knew how much uncle Larry had done for us, and I didn't want to disappoint him, but he had to understand the hard times I was having. So, I started to explain my problems. I saw the expression on his face change. It was clear had never expected my reaction. He, who had never asked anything of anyone. From surprise, to bewilderment, to disappointment, I saw the changes, and still I couldn't stop talking!

Finally, he raised his hand, signaling me to stop my blabbering. Looking me straight in the eye, and with a shake of the head, he said, "Vito, if you wanna, . . . you do"! Then, he turned and left me there, dumbfounded! I never got another chance!

The subject was never brought up again, and he was the same towards me afterwards as he had been before, but I had been changed for life! That image has haunted me ever since. Of course, he was right! I could have, and I should have, helped him! When you really want to do something, you find a way to do it! All the other reasons and excuses are just a lot of bullshit!

This has been a very long-winded story for such a short phrase. Evidently, I don't have uncle Larry's gift for saying a lot with a few words. So, when faced with difficult decisions in your life, think of uncle Larry, and do what's right. Remember, "If you wanna, . . . you do".

Gregory gets even, a.k.a. A nerdy revenge

This happened many years later than my other stories, but I think it's a classic, and should be included.

The year is 1994-1995, and my son Greg and Mary are living in a condominium in Fullerton, California. Greg is working at Rockwell as an Engineer. He is awakened one morning, before dawn, by the loud sound of a broken car muffler. When it didn't go away, he got up to see why. It was the newspaper deliveryman. He had parked his car, and left it running, while he made the local deliveries. This was very annoying to Greg, but he understood and had empathy, so he went back to bed, and waited for the guy to leave. However, the following morning the same thing happened, and again the next day. With each day, Greg was losing some of his understanding and empathy, until it was all gone, to be replaced by a mounting amount of anger and resentment.

You and I, and maybe 99% of the universe, probably would have gotten up and said something to the man. No, not Greg! Now, you must understand that Greg doesn't back down from anyone, but he is not confrontational by nature. He doesn't like to make trouble for anyone, and prefers to be a go-along to get-along kind of guy. That is, normally. In this case, while being forced to stay awake, he began thinking of ways to get back at the deliveryman. It just so happened that at the time, he was attending college, after work, to get a second degree in Electrical Engineering. His head was full of circuits and diagrams, and he wondered if he could use his new knowledge in this case. He formed a plan, and it took about two weeks to put it into effect.

I don't want to get too technical, or I'll lose the flavor of the story, but I need to do some. Greg's intention was to lay a water-sprinkler trap for the man, set to go off when he was in the center of the zone. How to do that?

He got a small microphone, to record the arrival of the vehicle. The problem was, how to distinguish that particular car? Well, it had a broken muffler, so it had a unique sound. That unique sound was going to trip a device, that would then open the faucet, and feed the water into the sprinkler, which would then soak the man. That was the plan, but he needed to set the range of that noise. So, alone in his garage, with microphone and voltmeter, he started trying to duplicate the noise that a broken muffler would make. "Brrrrfumpf-pop-pop, Brrrumpf-pop-pop" Louder, softer, deeper, higher, he pitched the noises into the microphone, and recorded the one he felt was the closest to the real thing. Only one problem was left. He didn't want the sprinkler to go off too soon, so he had to estimate the time it would take for the man to park, leave his car, and get to the center of the sprinkler zone. Having made his calculations, he put in a time-delay, and set the trap.

The next morning, he was up and waiting. Mary knew nothing of what had been going on for the previous two weeks. She woke up to find Greg standing at the window in the dark, and wondered what was going on. He didn't know if it was going to work, so he told her there was nothing wrong, and she went back to sleep.

Well, as the guy on the "A-Team" said, "It's great when a plan comes together." The broken-muffler car approached, the man got out, with a bunch of papers to be delivered. Crossing the lawn, when he got to the exact center of the "kill" zone, the sprinkler went off, sopping him and the newspapers! He couldn't get out of there fast enough! Behind the window, Greg was grinning from ear to ear. Oh sure, there may have been a little guilt, but there was mostly joy at the perfect execution of the plan. It was worthy of a "Mission Impossible" episode.

After that night, Greg never heard the car again. Probably started parking on the other side of the complex.

Early Years

1930-1940

Church of ✠ St. Rocco
216—27th Street   Brooklyn, N. Y.

CERTIFICATE OF BAPTISM

This is to certify that Vito Sciancalepore
child of Ignazio and Maria Vernice
born on the 31 day of Oct 1930
was Baptized according to the Rite of the Roman Catholic Church
on the 7 day of Dec 30
by the Rev. Th. di Corcia
Sponsors { Domenico Gatti
{ Angela
DATE Dec. 7. 1930

I was born on Halloween, October 31, 1930. My mother gave birth at home, a three-story apartment house on 23rd Street, in Brooklyn, New York. I never knew the exact address, but I understand an elevated highway was built years later that ran right by the corner of the street, and the house was the 2nd or 3rd up the block, on the left side.

Brooklyn
21 April, 1931

At about the age of 18 months, we moved back to Italy. The most notable news of the time was the kidnapping of the Lindbergh baby. That's Charles Lindbergh, the guy who flew solo across the ocean in his plane "The Spirit of St. Louis". My mother told me people commented on how much I resembled the missing baby. Considering we were traveling, and leaving the country, I always wondered if there was really a resemblance, or if people were just being paranoid.

Arriving in Corato, we settled in the house my grandfather had built, and my father had paid for, on property that was my mother's dowry. If you visualize the town as a circle, then the building would be located along the diameter, just off the center. The exact address is Via Duomo 84. Visualizing Corato as a circle will be helpful later on, to understand some of the stories. The building had two stores on the ground floor, one on either side of the entrance. There were two apartments on the second floor, two on the third floor, and one on the fourth, which was where we stayed. It was a rooftop apartment with a large terrace, and very comfortable. We had running water and a regular toilet, which was a luxury, and needs to be explained.

CORATO is a town in the province of Bari, and is about thirty miles north of the city itself, and about ten miles inland from the Adriatic coast, at an elevation of about 500 feet. It was primarily a farming community, with a population of about 20-30 thousand people at the time. The numbers are just educated guesses. What is not a guess is that there was a severe shortage of plumbing, except in the newer buildings, or in the older buildings of the well to do.

Running water was available at public fountains sprinkled throughout the town, and a regular chore was to fill clay storage vases at home with water from these fountains. This required many trips, and usually waiting in line at the fountain for your turn. Some buildings had wells available underneath, but the water quality was good for cooking, not for drinking. At least, that's the way I remember it.

Toilets are totally another subject! It's a very gross topic, and you should be prepared before reading further. To skip it would be to misrepresent the way of life in the town, and a subject that was both serious and funny to its citizens. So, choose the proper time to read further, or go on to the next chapter. It's your decision.

Remember that we are talking about a relatively poor farming community. Apartments didn't have bathrooms as such, and a minimum number of light bulbs. Electricity was very expensive, and many people lived by the light of oil lamps. Going to the bathroom required a decision. Was it number 1 or number 2? If it was number one, then you headed for the urinal, usually stored under the bed, one on each side. Number 2 required that you go sit on a clay pot to do your business. They were shaped like very large inverted top hats, and you would sit on the brim. Since there was no formal bathroom, they could be stored anywhere. An uncle had his in a dark small closet under the stairs. Another had his in a dark sub cellar. Still another had his in the attic, where he also kept live chickens. They would sit on their roost, while you sat on yours, like a jury, passing sentence on what you were doing. My maternal grandparents had theirs in the kitchen, stored with the firewood. Uncle Amerigo used to joke that he could do what he had to do, and stir the meat gravy at the same time! Keep in mind, there was no toilet paper. Brown wrapping paper from the groceries was kept, and torn to fill the need. Rough stuff!

At night, it wasn't unusual for people to empty their urinals, from their balconies into the street. Once again, uncle Amerigo always recommended that if you went for a walk in the evening in the back streets, it would be a very good idea to keep whistling.

Every morning a water truck would wash down the streets, and sometime in the day another wagon would pass to collect the contents of the top hats. He would announce his coming by blowing on a bugle, which was a signal for the women to bring the clay pots out to be emptied and rinsed. I tell you, it was a sigh
t, to see women lined up on their doorstep, clay pots resting on hip, waiting their turn. Furthermore, since this was an all day job, it was entirely possible that this "honey wagon"[1] would pass during dinnertime. Time out would be called, and dinner resumed after the chore was completed. Far from being grossed out, it was an opportunity to make jokes about the situation. Maybe that was the best way to handle it.

As I said at the beginning, I needed to present this so as to give you a better picture of the goings-on of this town. I repeat, the well-to-do weren't subjected to this ordeal, and really made some terrible jokes at the expense of those

---

[1] "Honey Wagon" was a term I picked up many years later, while stationed with the army in Salzburg, Austria. There I saw the same metal carts of my childhood in Corato, spraying the contents over farmland, to act as fertilizer for the growing crops.

that were. To be truly fair, having a toilet went a long way towards being considered "well-to-do". We had a toilet, and were considered "Americani", and rich, if not snobby well-to-do.

*   *   *

<u>My first memory:</u> Considering the above, it's probably not surprising that my very first memory is of my father taking a pee! I remember following him into the bathroom, as tall as his knees, and looking up to see this fountain empty into the toilet. It was quite a show, since I've never forgotten it. I must have been about 2-3 years old, since I also remember my baby brother, about 2 years younger than me, and the apartment, which we did not live in very long. I have no idea what I looked like, other than the pictures taken of me at the time. I was very chubby, then I was very skinny, due to a very serious illness. Fortunately, I recovered.

Vito and mom—1932

My mother later told me that she thought she was going to lose me, and donated her best piece of jewelry to St. Anthony (or St Francis, I'm not sure) in an effort to save my life. I remember seeing the gold bracelet draped over the statue of the saint in the apartment, and she never wore it.

1933   1934

I don't have memories of my very early years, just scattered images. Watching my father leave on a train, sensing that he was not coming back, was also a big moment. I remember him coming back a few years later, and staying until after Mike was born, before leaving again, but I was older then, and handled it much better.

Playing with my first baby brother Michele is a forever memory. I loved him then, and I love him now, and I always looked up to him as if he was the big brother. He was a great kid; lovable, cheerful, super-intelligent, and easy-going. Well, easy-going until I pushed too hard. I only did it once! I don't remember what I did, but it ticked him off, and he jumped on my back and bit me between the shoulder blades! I couldn't shake him off! When I went crying to my mother, she told me that if he did, then I must have deserved it! I had to agree with her.

Unfortunately, we weren't destined to be together long. I was sick with a cough, and he kept sneaking into the bedroom to keep me company. He caught my cough, which then went into pneumonia, and we lost him a little after age 2, (Nov. 17, 1932-March 31, 1935). However, even when he was very sick, and wasting away, he was a treasure. I remember a day, and the picture is still vivid in my mind. I was sitting on the floor playing with toys, keeping him company while he sat in the high chair, with my mother trying to get him to eat something. He had lost weight, and didn't have the strength to stand on his own, and he saw that we were not very happy. In a very earnest voice, he said, "Mommy, don't worry. If I die, you'll have another Michele". I wasn't even five myself, but I was flabbergasted that he would say such a thing. My mother and I looked at each other, and we never forgot that moment.

He died shortly thereafter. While he was laid out, and people came to mourn, I got this vision that I could be reunited with him, if I could crawl under the dresser, and reach the back wall. There wasn't much space for me to crawl under, but I tried and tried, until my uncle Amerigo pulled me out and took me outside to console me. I took it very hard, and have missed him every day since. I've gone through the guilt period of wondering why him and not me, and have reassured myself that he in fact did come back, just as he prophesied, in the body of the second Michele. He is still in my prayers to this day, and I talk to him regularly, and look forward to the day when I'll be reunited with him again.

*   *   *

Amerigo Vernice (10/3/1913-4/14/1966)

My uncle Amerigo was my hero, and represented everything I wanted to be when I grew up. He was funny, handsome, knew everyone, and was known and liked by everyone. Most important, he liked me, and took me with him whenever possible. If he went to the movies with his friends, he'd take me along. Once he went to Trani with his friends, and took me along. We ate at a seashore restaurant called "Scoglio di Frisio", and I felt so special that he would spend so much time with me. It was the period after the loss of my brother, and since my father was in America, my uncle meant very much to me. I have tried to mold my character to be like his my whole life. He was my mother's baby brother, and my hero. Years later, to honor him, I added his name to mine when I was Confirmed.

Unfortunately, since Italy under Mussolini went to war against Ethiopia around 1937, my uncle was drafted for the service, and I wound up losing him also, but not permanently. He would find ways to come home on leave, or find other ways. His story is entertaining and worth telling.

Amerigo Vernice - 1939

Zio Amerigo in his Cavalry uniform.
Check out his helmet on the Table.

When Amerigo Vernice reported for duty, he of course charmed the interviewers, who proceeded to assign him to the snappiest division, the cavalry. He assured them he could ride a horse as if born on one, when in fact the only horses he was acquainted with were those that pulled the wagons, and even those from the safety of the wagon seat.

The training was fine, the uniform was great, and when he got around to actually having to mount a horse, he did so without difficulty. He had his picture taken in uniform, and sent it home. A very dashing young man, he thought he had it made! Then came reality! Sitting on a horse was fine, if the horse stood still. He even managed to hold his own if the horse walked slowly. So, he managed to fake his way through training, and would lead his horse away from any activity that required movement. This in itself was a problem because his horse seemed to have a mind of his own, and didn't always go where my uncle wanted him to go. Things came to a head one day, when the troops were out on the parade grounds, preparing to pass in review of the commanding officers. This was beyond my uncle's speed, so he had managed to steer his mount away from the area, and was planning to go hide somewhere until the parade was over. Then disaster struck! The trumpeter sounded the call to arms, and my uncle's mount, who was better trained than my uncle, responded. Off at a gallop he went to join the troops on the parade grounds. Initially, my uncle pulled on the reins, and tried change course, but the animal would have none of that. When the beast was in full gallop, my uncle realized he was in way over his head, and just held on for dear life. Across the parade grounds went horse and rider, in full view of the assembled cavalry companies, until they came to a stop in front of the commanding Colonel, with my uncle barely hanging on to the horse's neck. We never were told of what was said, but my uncle never had to sit on another horse. He cleaned the stables every day for the next couple of months, until he was reassigned.

This time they got it right. He was sent to the motor pool to be a truck driver. He enjoyed that, and sometimes took advantage. When sent on errands with his truck, he would detour so he could pass through Corato and visit with us. Considering that he was posted fifty miles away, it was quite a detour. One night, my mother and I were on the terrace, when my uncle drove up with a truckload of soldiers that he was supposed to be transporting in the opposite direction, all whooping and hollering. He told them to stay there while he visited with us for a couple of hours, and it's a reflection of how everybody liked him, that they all did as they were told in good humor. They were all happy to be in on the "escape". I'm sure these kinds of escapades didn't endear him to his commanding officers, and could be the reason why, when he eventually got to the war front in Albania, he was assigned to transport truckloads of dynamite to the front lines. Not a healthy assignment!

One way or another, he made it through the war for the next six years, until Italy surrendered, and changed sides, I think in 1943. Unfortunately, when that happened, my uncle was stationed in Naples, together with the German army. One day, the Germans were allies, the next they were the enemy. The war wasn't over, and my uncle found himself unable to rejoin the Italian army. Confused, not knowing who was friend or foe, he decided that enough was enough, and went home. However Corato was 250 miles away, on the other side of the mountains. It took him over three weeks to walk home, hiding in the road gutters by day, and walking at night, staying clear of any other human being, not trusting anyone. He wasn't alone, because there were many others that were disoriented like him, going back to their own hometowns. Since they were living off the land as they traveled, they had a common enemy. Farmers patrolled their properties with shotguns, and shot at anything that moved. Eventually, he got home, and reported for duty at the local camp. He was immediately arrested and thrown in prison, and there was the threat that he was going to be shot for desertion in wartime. Fortunately, he was able to talk his way out it, and at war's end, received an honorable discharge. However, he had lost eight years of his life, and had nothing to show for it. Nothing that was remotely comparable to the benefits available to American servicemen when they returned home. The only thing they couldn't take away was his personality, which remained the same for his whole life, and made him a joy to be with, in good times and in bad. He was a truly wonderful human being, and my favorite person, right behind my mother.

*   *   *

I really don't know if the loss of my brother was the reason why I misbehaved, or if that was my normal character, but it seems I was always in trouble. The nuns advised my mother that I was a handful, and she was forced to take me out of Catholic school and enroll me in public school in the second grade. I wasn't destructive. I just didn't respond well to the strict discipline, and I didn't like to study. My favorite pastime was getting a girl classmate to giggle, for which we would be punished. We would be sent to the Mother Superior's office, and spent the rest of the day there, sitting in chairs at opposite sides of her office, in silence, while she worked. The girl's name was Luisa DiBenedetti, and she was my girlfriend, even though we never saw each other outside of school.

It didn't get any better in public school. I would play hookey from school, and walk around the outskirts of town, called the "Stramurale"(or "outside the walls"), until it was time to go home. Once I bought a pack of cigarettes, and smoked the whole pack before I went home. No, I didn't inhale, just puffed away, because I couldn't take any home with me. It was the only time I ever lit a cigarette, but I did other things. I learned to trace my mother's signature, and signed notes to the teacher at school, excusing my absences. However, when I was absent for a whole week, the teacher was concerned, and came to the house, and it was all over. I can't even blame anyone else, because I did these things alone. I always wondered how I was able to get away with it for so long, especially with the writing and signing of the notes. I always assumed it was due to my cleverness, but with age came a more reasonable answer. Only the rich had telephones, so any checking up would have to be done in person. Also, many people couldn't read or write. So, a note written shakily in an infantile manner was perfectly normal, and would not cause suspicion.

I was friendly with everyone, but was very comfortable by myself. However, there were times when company was needed. For instance, we used to charge our groceries, and my mother would sometimes send me to do the shopping. The grocery store had an open barrel of small fried silverfish, packed in vinegar, and the smell made my mouth water. So, I decided to have a party. I bought some of the silverfish, some fresh prosciutto and provolone, some fresh bread, and then invited a couple of friends to share it with me. We went to a local piazza, near a water fountain, and partied! It was such a great experience, I decided to do it again, and then again. Unfortunately, it happened on the day my mother went to pay the bill at the grocer, and was informed of my recent purchases. So, when I returned home, I found my mother and my uncle Amerigo waiting for me, and I felt that something was not right! When my uncle asked me to open my mouth, so he could smell my breath, I knew the jig was up. The smell of vinegar from the fried silverfish was still deliciously rolling around my mouth, and I had to confess everything. Curiously, I didn't get a beating or anything. As a matter of fact, I never was spanked for my bad behavior.

1936   JULY - 1936

Another time, while looking through my mother's desk, I came across two one-dollar bills. I knew what they were because I had accompanied my mother to the store, where she would exchange the dollar for Italian lira. I took the two dollars, went to the store, and cashed one dollar, which at the time was worth eleven lira. The owner knew me, so I had no problem, even though I was only seven years old. Now, armed with all this money, what could I do? Of course, I went to buy candy. I bought mints, caramels, licorice drops, and all sorts of other things my eyeballs desired. My pockets were full, and I hadn't spent all that money yet. What to do? Well, I decided to enjoy what I had bought, and would worry about the rest later. I proceeded to walk around town, eating my booty. I hadn't finished eating what I had bought, and was feeling rather sick, when I realized I had a problem. I had candy left, I had liras left, and I still had a dollar left! I hadn't realized that in my wandering, I had wound up near my apartment house. As I stood on the corner, not comfortable at all, staring at the dollar that I had left, wondering what to do, I felt a presence over my right shoulder. I looked up to see my uncle Amerigo looming over me. I took off like a shot, and I ran without looking back until I got tired, and then sat down to review my miserable day, and how I could get out of it. After a while, I decided to throw myself at the mercy of the court! I made my way back to the house, rang the bell, and asked my mother to lower the basket on the rope. Since we lived on the top floor, it was a convenient way to bring things up without doing the stairs. I put all the leftover candy and money in there, and then left to walk the streets some more. When I got up enough courage, I went home, to face my mother and my uncle. Once again, I got away with it! Now I realize that they were more amused than upset with me, but then I wondered why they didn't smash me.

One day, a large trunk was delivered to our door. My father had sent it from America with a friend who had come to visit his family. There must have been at least ten pairs of shoes in it, plus some other things for my mother, but most of the space was filled with toys for me. Looking back, maybe my father was trying to help us recover after the loss of my brother. Anyway, there was a big metal model airplane, battery powered, and the propellers turned (jets hadn't been invented yet), and the cabin lights went on inside the plane, and I could look inside through the little windows, and see all the people sitting in their chairs. I had never seen anything like it. Also, there was a full size riding car, pedal driven, also with batteries that made the headlights go on and off. It also had a gear shift which didn't really attach to any gears, but made clicking noises when I moved it up and down as if I was really changing gears. It was fire engine red, and there was nothing like it in town. I used to pedal it on the streets of Corato, accompanied by uncle Amerigo. He enjoyed taking me to the gasoline pump, and making believe he was filling up my gas tank.

There was also a tricycle in the trunk, but it was taken apart. My grandfather volunteered to put it together, took the parts to his office, but never got around to doing it. When I got tired of the other toys, I went to his office, which was a dark dingy place in the back street behind our house, and pestered him until he reassembled it. He brought it up to our apartment, and I took it out on the terrace to try it out. It was only when I started to ride it that I noticed my grandfather had mounted the pedals side by side, instead of one up and one down. I didn't want to tell anybody, because I knew he would take it away to fix it, and I would never see it again. So I tried to ride it, pushing on both pedals at the same time. Bad idea! It was OK going straight, and I built up some speed, but as soon as I turned, the tricycle toppled, and I fell over it. Unfortunately, the metal edge of the pedal made a serious gash in my right knee. My mother had to call the doctor, who came to the house, and stitched up the wound, but not before he removed the "bad blood". This was done by putting leaches, which he carried in a glass jar in his medical bag, around the wound to suck up the blood. I was fascinated watching, and I think I wound up getting six stitches. I still have the scar as a reminder. Funny, but I don't remember ever riding that tricycle again.

Not all recollections are amusing. One time, my mother left me playing on the terrace. I was playing with a belt, when I dropped it over the railing. So, I climbed over the railing, picked up the belt, and proceeded to walk back and forth on the little parapet, not aware that with one step I would fall to the street below. My first clue came when my mother came back to the terrace. I had never seen that look in her eye! Also, she had never spoken to me so calmly, asking me to just stand still, and why was she walking so slowly towards me? Fortunately, while I was wondering all these things, she got to the railing, and I felt an iron grip on both my arms, much stronger than anything I had ever felt before, and I knew I must have done something wrong! I honestly didn't have a clue! My only defense is I'm pretty sure I was not yet five years old at the time, because my memory is that my mother had gone in to check on my brother.

Sometimes things went bad through no fault of my mine, like the time a neighbor finally let me walk his prized German shepherd dog, after I had been pestering him for weeks. How was I to know the dog was in heat. All I knew was that, as I took the dog around the corner, another big dog jumped on him. The two of them were taller than I was, so I left them there, and went to tell the owner. I had never heard such curse words! When he went, and found he couldn't separate the two dogs, even after throwing buckets of cold water on them, I heard even more variations of those curse words. The man was a good guy, and I wanted him to like me again. So, some time later, I overheard him telling my mother that he wasn't driving his automobile because it needed to be fixed. Something was wrong with the motor. I saw my chance to do something good. So during the time people used to take an afternoon nap, I went where the auto was garaged, and proceeded to fix his motor. I pulled out every wire I could, and was very proud of myself. When I returned home, and my mother asked what I had been doing, because I was all dirty from oil stains, I proudly told her what I had done. Strangely, her reaction was not what I had expected. I'm sure it cost her a pretty penny to undo my "fixing up".

* * *

"Mikey" is born

About this time, my father returned from America, my mother got pregnant, and my second baby brother Michele was born on Sept. 23rd, 1938. I know this now, but at the time, it came as a complete surprise. I remember that I was playing in front of our building, when my father came out and asked me, "Would you like to come upstairs to see your new brother, who has just arrived?" (that's the way he said it to me). Of course I was excited, and followed him upstairs, but I was very puzzled. I had been playing by the front entrance all the while, and I couldn't figure out how, if my new baby brother had just arrived, how did he get past me without me seeing him? I never asked for an explanation, so I don't know how long I was left to wonder. My first impression of Michele was that he was so small, but cried very loud for such a little package, and I couldn't make out his face because it was mostly an open mouth. In truth, I don't remember him crying after that first time. He was a calm baby, and I didn't even know he was around. He was not as animated as I remembered my first brother, but he was lovable.

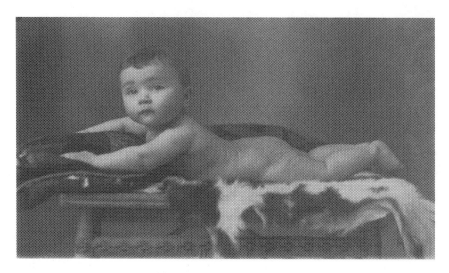

Michele II   1938

Now, you would think that with my father around, I would behave better. You would be wrong! I would embarrass my father, as I had my mother. A friend of his invited him out to his country home to eat barbecued wild rabbits, and my father took me along. It was a long bike ride to the outskirts of town, and I was very hungry when we got there. Unfortunately, the host had invited too many people for the rabbits he had to share. That wasn't my fault! All I knew was I had gulped down my portion and I was still very hungry. So, I proceeded to raise my hand to ask for some more. My father tried to stop me from doing so by pinching my leg under the table. I promptly yelled out, and when my father's friend asked what was the matter, I told everyone that my father had just pinched me because he didn't want me to ask for any more meat. I saw my father turn red, and figured that at some point I was going to get it good. The host was even more embarrassed, but assured that there was plenty of meat to go around, and proceeded to give me another healthy portion. Now I was happy, and if I were going to get a spanking, it would be on a full stomach. Fortunately for me, by the time we got home, my father saw the humor in the situation, and put the blame where it belonged, on his friend.

Ahhhhh, poetic justice! A few weeks later, I accompanied my father out to his friend's place again. This time my father was going to build him a new barbecue pit, maybe to make up for my previous misbehavior. I had all day to play around with his son, and accompanied him into the pen to feed the goats. Unfortunately, the billy goat was as big as me, and I guess didn't like me. He charged me, and butted me on my rear end. I didn't know what to do, so I just stood there with my backside to the goat. He kept backing up, charging, and butting me again and again, until the other boy came and pulled him away. Now, I'm sure it had nothing to do with it, but I also drank a lot of well water that day. In any case, within a few days I became sick with typhoid, which laid me up for couple of months, requiring daily injections. It turned out OK, because my father started giving me money: One Lira for an injection in the rear, and two Liras for one in the arm.

I earned enough money from my injections, so my father bought me a train set from part of the money, and set it up on the floor at the foot of the bed, where I could watch it go round and round. Of course, in those days, it wasn't electric, and the engine spring needed to be wound up, but it was a great joy to me. My joy, however, was short lived! My aunt, on my father's side, came to visit, together with her two sons. They were farmers, and the kids were a couple years older than I. They had never had a train like the one I had, and I'm sure were very jealous. So, they "accidentally" happened to step on my train with their hobnailed shoes, totally destroying it, and all that money earned from all those painful injections. They didn't offer to replace it, I never forgot it, and a few months later I got even.

When they came to visit again, I was healthy. While the adults visited, I suggested we could go out on the large terrace, and play "horse and carriage". They had never played this game, and I proceeded to teach them. After running ropes from behind the neck, over the shoulders to the front, and then under the armpits to the rear, they now were the horses, and I was holding the reins. For the carriage, each of them pulled a chair behind them, and I followed, holding the reins, and pulling right or left to direct where they would go. In addition, I also carried a whip, made from another length of rope tied to a stick, which was used to "prod" the horses to go faster. Needless to say, the horses never galloped fast enough, and I whipped them mercilessly, until they quit, and went crying to their mother. I told them it was just a game, but I don't know if they ever believed me. I know my mother never did.

Another instance revolving around food. Once again, with my father, I accompanied him to hire someone to do a job for him. He lived in a one-room apartment at street level, and we arrived just at the time when he was preparing something to eat. Now, you must know we're talking about a poor person here, and he was frying five or six onion scallions in a pan, to eat with a piece of bread. That would be his main meal of the day, but I wasn't aware of any of it. The sweet odor from those scallions made my mouth water, and when the poor guy invited us to share his dinner, I promptly sat down and ate most of it. My father of course was saying no, that we had to leave, but it was too late. While the two of them watched, I ate. Boy, was it good! My father scolded me severely, but he couldn't insult the man by paying for the food. He did pay him generously for the work later, but that was after the guy had gone hungry for a day. Through all of these things, I never saw myself as a bad kid, and nobody ever said I was a bad kid. As a matter of fact, outside of my cousins, everybody liked me.

Speaking of my cousins, I would like to share a story of a day I spent with them, and to thank God once again for being born as me.

My parents thought it would be a good idea if I spent a day working with my farming relatives, and they agreed to take me with them. I was up at 3:00AM, and at their house by 4:00AM. They had already hitched the horse to the wagon, and were waiting for me. My uncle, aunt (my father's sister), two cousins, and myself, mounted on the cart, and headed out of town for their field. They lit a lantern, and hung it under the cart, so others would see us on the road. The horse knew the way, so we didn't do much except wrap ourselves up in a blanket, and try to get some more sleep. It must have taken at least an hour to get to their field, and it was still pitch black when we got there. The early morning air was chilly, and my bones were stiff from the cart ride. The back roads were potted, and the open cart had no springs. They unhitched the horse from the wagon, started an open fire to warm us up, then picked some ripe olives from the trees, and threw them in the fire. When the fire consumed, they pulled out the burnt olives, blew off the ashes, and ate hot olives and bread. I had never tasted this before, and got sick to my stomach. Many years would pass before I would eat another olive. By this time, daylight was breaking, and it was time to go to work. We had come to pick the olive trees, and spent the whole day doing that. First, large sheets would be spread under an olive tree, so as to catch all the olives that would drop from the branches. Then, my uncle and aunt would go from branch to branch, with the help of a ladder, and strip the olives, so that they would fall unto the sheets. We, the kids, would pick the olives up, and put them in wicker baskets. When all the baskets were filled, we would transfer the olives into sacks, making sure to remove any leaves first. This went on all day. We took a break to eat, but I don't remember what. There was nothing but the field, and olive trees, so it must have been something brought from home. A short afternoon nap was customary, but I don't remember it. We continued until it started to get dark, then hitched up the horse again, loaded all the sacks unto the wagon, climbed on top of the sacks, and headed home. It was dark when we got back. Once again they unhitched the horse, and told me to bring it into its stall, which was under the house they lived in. I remember holding those leather reins, being not much taller than the horse's knees, and wondering how I was going to get that big monster to move. Fortunately, the horse knew what to do, and dutifully went into his stall, and began munching on hay. My uncle came in, and rubbed him down with a stiff brush, and finally my day was over! I had been tired from before daybreak, and this had been my day from Hell. Never would I put myself in a position to have another day like it. Truth to tell, I'm sure my relatives didn't think very much of me, and probably laughed at what a sissy I was. I admire their work ethic, but it was not my world, thank God.

My father returned to America, and we followed, in the summer of 1939. Europe was at war, and they must have figured it would be safer for us to be in the U.S. I wasn't aware of the war, except that I knew my uncle Amerigo was away. Also, I had my "Balilla" uniform, a miniature version of Mussolini's "Black shirts". Periodically, the teachers would take us out of class, to march with small wooden rifles on the grounds in back of the school. I still didn't like school, and used to have extra study after school at the teacher's house, for which my mother paid extra.

I don't think I was stupid. I was fine with math, but didn't have a clue about history or geography. For instance, one day the teacher called me to the front of the class. There was a large map hanging in front of the blackboard, and he asked me to point to a certain river. I didn't have the slightest idea of what he was talking about, but he was standing there, holding a long wooden pointer, and I needed to do something before it came crashing down on me. So, I put my finger somewhere on the gigantic map, and cringed, waiting for the whipping. When it didn't come, I looked up to see the teacher smiling at me, obviously pleased, and figuring his after-school lessons were paying dividends. No such luck—I had just made a wild guess, and hit the lottery! Now, we were both happy, and I started back to my seat. The teacher, however, wanted to show off, and asked me to point to another river. Big mistake! I wasn't about to take another chance, so I just pointed to the river I had previously identified. He patiently advised me that he was asking for another river, but I just kept pointing to the same spot as before. He finally realized it was futile, and told me to go back to my desk, but at least I didn't get hit. Many years later (I was twenty years old), I ran into this teacher, Professore Cinone, who told me that all the whippings he had given me were because he really liked me. I told him I wished he hadn't like me so much, since it didn't seem to have done any good anyway.

I had started school with the Cappuccine nuns. They kicked me out after two years. Public school was no better, and I hadn't finished the 3rd grade when we fortunately left for the States.

My last remembrance before leaving, is of a day spent picking grapes. This was so much different from my olive-picking day.

My mother had some cousins that were picking grapes to make wine, and we went to help out. When we arrived, we were given a wicker basket and a knife, and told to go down a row, cut the grapes from the vines, and bring the full baskets back to the main clearing. There were about 30 people altogether, all happy and joking while working. In the clearing was a very large tub, and we would dump the grapes into it. Then barefoot men and women would stomp on the grapes, sometimes more than knee deep. The day was fun and passed very quickly. In the late afternoon, the men continued to work, but the women got together by the farmhouse and started cooking spaghetti and a fresh tomato sauce. Since there were so many people, they set up a long table outside. Then all work stopped and everybody got together around the long table. There was no electricity, so everybody took their battery-powered lamp from the bicycles they had come on, and shone it on the table. These, together with the light from some lanterns, made for a memorable scene, and the good humor completed the picture. I tasted my first pomegranate that day, and was fascinated by its ruby-like fruit, and how they all lined up like miniature teeth. It didn't seem like work at all.

*   *   *

That's about all my memories of my first years in Italy. There are others, like spending days at the cemetery, keeping my grandfather company, watching him work chiseling marble, and wandering alone among the graves in the dark, waiting for him to give me a ride on his bicycle back to town. . . . Or the summer we rented a room on the water in Trani. It had no running water, so my mother kept a big bottle of water on the windowsill. Unfortunately, she also kept a big bottle of olive oil on the same sill. One day, coming in all sweated and thirsty, I must have taken at least ten gulps before I realized it wasn't water. . . . Or the following summer, that we rented a room on the water in Bisceglie, and I was riding a bike, lost my balance, and fell in front an oncoming horse and wagon. The horse stepped over me, and the wheels missed me. I didn't get even a scratch!

I'm sure you've noticed that all of my memories are either solitary ones, or with my family, and it was fine with me. It's just that nothing memorable happened with my friends, with one exception. His name was Felice Fiore, and we met while I was recuperating from typhoid (after the goat-butting incident). My parents rented a place in the country outside of Corato, figuring the air would speed up my recovery. It was isolated, with no electricity. We made friends with the people on the next property, and would spend the evenings together by candlelight, until it was time to go to bed. Felice and I were always together, finding things to do to amuse us. In the daytime, we would go up and down the country roads, picking and eating fruits, or collecting a pot full of snails from between the rocks that made up the walls separating the properties. These would later be cooked and eaten. Nights, we would listen to the adult conversation until it was time to go to bed. Then, one of the parents would accompany the child to bed with one of the candles, and come back. One night, we were at Felice's place, and when it was time to go to bed, his mother took him inside, put him to bed, and returned. At this point it's necessary that I mention a couple of things. First, the nights were very warm, and that's why we stayed up as late as possible. Also, we were always at the mercy of some very large bugs, that kept slapping into us. They were totally harmless, but Felice was terrified of them. Anyway, we were getting ready to leave, when Felice comes running out screaming, totally naked, crying about the "Vurruque" that were in his bedroom. Him jumping up and down, naked and screaming, was the funniest sight I had ever seen, and I would never let him forget it.

As a matter of fact, twenty years later, I was running the nightclub "La Lampara", when Felice came in. I hadn't seen him in years, and he had become a big deal in politics. He had come from Rome, and was accompanied by a large group of local politicians, all fawning over him. We embraced, and I set up his group with a few tables. When

I saw that he was in his full glory, holding court with his cronies, I went over, and in a very serious tone, asked Felice if he wanted to move his group indoors, because I had just received an alert that an attack of "vurruque" was on the way. The look he gave me was priceless. Later, he took me aside, and said "Vito, please understand that I'm a very serious person now, and can't afford to be embarrassed in public." We looked each other in the eye, and then must have laughed for ten minutes, convincing his buddies that he really wasn't all that serious a person.

Coming to America—

1939

I don't remember the exact date we left, but I know that I hadn't finished the 3rd grade, and it was warm. My best guess is it was April 1939. My mother rented a closed carriage to take us to the Trani railroad station, about a

45 minute ride, and I sat outside, on top with the driver. It must have seemed like a lifetime to him, because he told my mother when we arrived, that I hadn't shut up for a minute during the whole trip.

From Trani, we took a train to Naples, and a taxi to the docks. I had never been to a big city before, and was impressed by the hustle and bustle. All the automobiles, the trolley cars, and all the people! The one thing that stands out the most is seeing a vendor with a pushcart, selling bananas. What was odd was that the bananas were stored under glass, and the vendor was wearing a white gown and gloves, so he wouldn't touch the fruit with his fingers. Now, I had been eating bananas in Corato, especially when I was sick, and I knew they were expensive, but this looked like something I had to have, and of course my mother got it for me. What a let-down. It didn't taste any different than the ones in Corato.

We boarded the "REX", and went to our cabin in tourist class, at the bottom of the ship. In those days, there was a 1st class, a cabin class, and tourist class. For me, it was heaven! I had never seen such luxury! A cabin to ourselves, with bunk beds! There was a restaurant, with white tablecloths, and fancy waiters to serve us. All I wanted to eat, and free movies afterwards. I really didn't know where we were going, although I'm sure I had been told a million times, and I really didn't care! I had all this, and no school. What a life!

Unfortunately, about two days out of port, Mike got sick. My mother took him to the infirmary, but she remained there with him, having her own bed. At least that's what she told me, that she had to care for the baby, and I had to take care of myself. It's taken me all these years to realize that she was not well! Otherwise, she could have left the baby with the doctors and nurses and visited all day long. Obviously, she didn't want me to know there was anything wrong with her, and used Mike as an excuse. Pretty sneaky, mom!

After about 30 seconds of disappointment, I adjusted to my independence. I had the cabin all to myself! I loved the rocking of the ship, and boy did it rock! I had to put myself crossways so I wouldn't fall out of the top bunk, and was rocked to sleep. After washing up in the morning, I would go up for breakfast. The waiters knew the situation, and took great care of me. This, plus the fact that most of the other passengers were seasick in their cabins, gave me the run of the ship. I took frequent runs to the infirmary, to make sure everything was OK, and then off exploring some new staircase. I didn't spend too much time outside on the open deck. I noticed there was just enough space under the railing for me to slip through, and fall in the ocean, and the way the ship was rolling, I saw myself losing my balance, and going overboard. It was also very windy outside, and a gust took the beret off my head. As I saw my hat fly off the ship, and into the ocean with those big waves, I pictured that it was me, and I never went outside again. So, I visited the kitchen, the engine room (from which they shooed me away), and talked to the sailors. No friends. I was just happy by myself. Eating, sleeping, watching movies, and exploring. The ten-day trip passed pretty quickly.

We arrived at night, so I never got to see the postcard view of Manhattan Island. My father and uncle Larry picked us up, and brought us to uncle Larry's apartment, where we met aunt Clara, and shared the living quarters for a few months, until we got our own place.

If I thought Naples was busy, New York was just another world! Big cars, big buildings, and so many of them, but what really caught my eye were the neon signs! Especially the sequential ones, like a moving arrow that pointed to the entrance of something. I couldn't take my eyes off them.

My next culture shock was the traffic light! The day after arriving, my father took me out to show me the neighborhood, which was East 148th Street and Morris Ave (there's a hospital there now). When we had to cross 149th Street, we waited for the light to change, and my father explained how it worked. When we did get the green light, I refused to budge. I would not believe that just because a light turns red, those monster cars would stop. I gave them a life of their own, waiting to eat me if I stepped into the street.

Finally, I saw others crossing, and decided to trust my father. I held on to his hand for dear life, and that was the biggest street I have crossed in my life, although it was only two lanes.

The next surprise was chewing gum. My uncle Larry gave me a stick, told me to chew it, but not to swallow. How silly. You only put things in your mouth if you intend to eat

them, and spit it out only if you can't chew it, or it tastes awful. It didn't make sense to chew something sweet, and then spit it out, but I quickly adapted to the "chu-gum".
The language wasn't a problem, at least not at first. All the adults we came in contact with spoke Italian, as well as the storeowners when we went shopping. The kids in the neighborhood didn't speak Italian, but were willing to teach me English. I sensed the words they were feeding me were very bad words, and that I couldn't trust them. So, like in Italy, I was more-or-less on my own, which was fine with me.

The language became a problem when I started school. My mother and Aunt Clara accompanied me to the principal's office to enroll in public school. Trying to evaluate what class to put me in, he asked if I could do long division, and how many numbers I could divide by. I told him by as many as he wanted. Surprised, he gave me a few problems, which I processed correctly. So, he decided to put me in the third grade, which was the grade I had left in Italy.

Wonderful! Except, duhhhhhhhh, I didn't understand a word the teacher was saying! It took a few days for the teacher to realize this, after which I was transferred to the second grade. No better luck there, so eventually I found myself where I should have been in the first place, in kindergarten, learning basic words. That was fine with me, except the desks were made for a six-year-old, and I could barely fit into one.

I enjoyed kindergarten, and learned very quickly. I was the smartest kid in the class, and always got gold stars for my work. The other kids also were awed by how much I ate, and lunchtime was show time for them. While they nibbled on crackers and jelly sandwiches, I would open my brown paper bag, and pull out a big Italian bread sandwich, which seemed almost as big as they were, filled with all kinds of stuff! I enjoyed showing off how much I could eat!

At the end of the semester, I was ready to move on, but my teacher wouldn't promote me to the first grade. My understanding of the language was coming along fine, but I was hesitant to speak. I especially refused to say the word "the"! I could do "Duhhh", but "the" required me to stick the tongue outside my teeth for the "th" sound, and this I wouldn't do! It was like sticking your tongue out at people! The teacher wouldn't compromise, and had my mother and Aunt Clara come to class on the last day. When tears didn't work, I finally said the "the" word, and I moved on.

Uncle Larry took me to the first movie in America, and it was a Western, starring Tom Mix. This was right down my alley, and I went as often as I could, by myself. Not only did I enjoy myself, but it also helped me learn the language much faster. Any movie was fine, so long as there was action.

In the following year, I made it back to the third grade, but I never made up the missing year. However, I did chip my two front teeth, which have remained that way to this day! While walking to school one morning, I was looking at two girls my age also walking to school, but on the other side of the street. Not watching where I was going, I bumped into something. Thinking it was a person, I put my arms around him, and said "I'm sorry". I quickly realized that the person was a fat metal pole. My first thought was to look around to see if anyone had seen me make a fool of myself. I was relieved to find no one behind me, and even when I spit out a couple of pieces of my two front teeth, I was thankful.

So did my mind operate as I completed my first decade on Earth.

* * *

1940-1949

Note—*This whole period was characterized by "first time" experiences, which is normal for all growing children, but is of no help to the person going through it, which in this case would be me.*

Living quarters were cramped, so we quickly found an apartment a couple of blocks away on 150th Street. It was on the 2nd or 3rd floor, small, and noises came through the walls from the apartments below, above, and on either side. School was out, and it was very hot inside the apartment. Fortunately, we had a firehouse directly across the street, and the firemen would open up the hydrant for us kids during the day. We used all kinds of gadgets to get a good spray from the hydrant's cool water, and had fun seeing who could make the tallest spray, or the furthest, or whatever. When cool, and tired of those games, we would lay in wait for an unsuspecting motorist to pass by, sitting innocently on the sidewalk, next to the running hydrant. When he came within range, the best "spray" guy among us would quickly block the flow of water with a big piece of wood, and get the car with the spray. If we were lucky, sometimes the car window would be open, and we would hit the jackpot. Of course, the motorist was never happy, and we all scattered. This usually resulted in the hydrant being shut off for a couple of days, which we spent alternately talking about how we "got that guy", and begging the firemen to turn the hydrant back on.

Nights were hot, and we spent as much time as possible on the iron fire escape outside our windows. Fortunately, my mother had a better idea. She talked my father, uncle Larry, and another friend, into renting a house for the summer. So, we soon found ourselves sharing a house in Throggs Neck, a couple of blocks from Long Island Sound. What fun! In the water all day (it was rocky, but we wore rubber shoes), and a lot of people (or so it seemed) eating together in the evening, outside under a grape arbor.

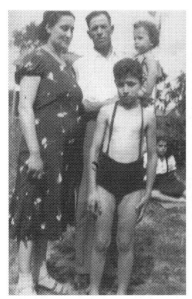

Vito and Mike-1940

Family at Throggs Neck-1940

My father and uncle Larry couldn't come every night, because it was too far from work, but came for long weekends. On these occasions, we would generally go out in the evening. Sometimes to the bar-restaurant nearby, where the grownups would enjoy a couple of beers, and I would spend money at the electric rifle range, trying to hit the target in the puppet's shoulder as he moved across the stage, which would then make him turn, and go the other way. I could stay there for hours.

Other times, we would walk to "German Stadium". It was a catering hall, which also served as a dance hall, and we would sit and listen to the music, and watched people dance while little kids slid across the floor, and grownups would exchange sandwiches by throwing them across from table to table. Years later, they became known as "Football Weddings". The people at "German Stadium" were mostly German (duhhhh), or so you would think. Europe was at war, and I was told years later that a lot of the people there were probably FBI or undercover government agents, looking for German spies.

I didn't know any of this stuff. I was enjoying all these new experiences. I had my first Coca-Cola. Reaching through the ice in the metal bin to find the coldest soda underneath was an adventure I looked forward to on those hot afternoons after the beach. Playing horseshoes with the grownups, and watching them tease each other during meals was better than the movies. I also enjoyed walking with my father while he picked "la ruca" from the grasses, to make a salad for dinner. It looked like wild grass to me, but Aida insists it's the Dandelion plant without the flower, because she also helped her father pick it.

Mike Mastromauro was the friend of the family (called "u nasone—big nose-" for obvious reasons, but never to his face). One weekend he came with his car, a two-seater, with a rumble seat in the back. I was so impressed with the car that he offered to let me drive it. Of course, he was kidding, but I didn't know that. I took the keys and jumped in the car. To his credit, he let me try, and even told me what to do. After I had stalled a couple of times, and gone maybe fifteen feet, we both agreed I should wait a while. It was a great summer!

Back home, my parents realized we needed a new place, so we moved over another couple of blocks to 684 Courtland Ave, between 153rd and 154th Street. It was a three-story house, with the top two floors over a small fruit and vegetable store run by the landlady Eugenia and her husband. They lived behind the store, and the married daughter/son lived above us. The apartments were set back, and the area above the store was our terrace, from which we could people-watch in the evenings.

The apartment itself had a large bedroom for my parents, a very large kitchen area that also had a kerosene stove for heat, and two small bedrooms for Mike and myself. There was also a back yard where some people would plant vegetables, but I don't think we ever did. Maybe that's where Eugenia got her vegetables.

Uncle Larry also moved to another nicer apartment on 151st Street, and we would see each other regularly.

My First Fight—

I walked to my new public school on 157th Street. I still had no friends, and it still didn't bother me. That is, except for the times when the other kids would pick on me. Make no mistake, kids picked on each other, but I was one of the few that had no buddies. The others were German, Irish, and whatever, but they were born here. I was the "Wop" or "Guinee", and the name Sciancalepore didn't help any.

To be fair, I really didn't have anything in common with the other kids, except for age. I hadn't learned about any of the things kids talked about, which was mostly about sports, and I didn't know how to play any of their games. Also, we had been moving from place to place, and I had not been in any one class for very long while I was trying to catch up to my age group.

It's easy for me to see and say that now, but at the time, it was a problem. Most of the kids left me alone, but there was a little group of about six that bullied the other kids, but especially me or some innocent "Jew-boy". Lunch breaks in the schoolyard were manageable because there was usually a teacher on hand. Going home after school was another matter. They would wait and follow me, taunting and saying things I don't remember, except that they were not nice! I was intimidated, and never said a word. Intimidated Hell! I was scared, and I didn't know what to do or say. I had only been in one fight in Corato, and that one didn't really count.

I had been in line at the public water fountain, waiting to fill my bucket for my grandparents' water jars, when an older kid cut in line ahead of me. I started yelling at him, and he promptly hit me over the head with his clay jug. Fortunately, the jug broke. When he saw that all he had left was the handle, the boy started crying and ran home. I knew why he was crying. Boy, was he gonna get it when he got home! I was so pleased with myself that I didn't even realize I was bleeding all over my face, until I got home with my full pail of water. Turned out OK though, because I was never sent for water after that.

As I was saying, I didn't know what to do, and my silence only made them madder, until one day they blocked my way, and there was no way around them. One of them started pushing me backwards, and I felt something against the back of my knees, took a quick look, and saw another kid on his hands and knees behind me, so that when his buddy pushed me again, I would fall over him. Without thinking, when the next push came, I grabbed the guy's shirt, and twisted around, so that he fell over his own buddy. At this point, another kid jumped on my back, and wrapped his arms around my neck. I don't know where the bright idea came from, but I jumped up in the air, and fell backwards. When I hit the ground, I had the nice cushion on my back, but he didn't. I heard the crack of his head on the sidewalk, and he let go of me. I got up, and the kids still standing didn't do anything. I had never let go of my schoolbag, and I walked past them without saying a word. My legs were shaking, and I braced for the next attack. It never came. I kept walking, and didn't look back, so I have no idea what was going on behind me. What I do know is that they never bothered me again!

I go into these details because they were my first experiences, and I still remember them vividly.

*   *   *

Finally, I started making some friends "on the block". Where you lived was "the block", and you spent almost all your time there. It was almost self-sufficient, having almost all the stores for everyday shopping. In order, from left to right, we had across the street from us, all the shops. The A&P and fruit store were on the corners of 153rd street, followed by a Jewish candy store, a German delicatessen, a bread bakery, an Irish bar, an Italian barber, and a butcher. On our side we had the Sisto Funeral parlor on one corner, and a hardware store on the other. We even had a junkman that stabled his horse and wagon in the yard adjoining our property. Yes, horse and wagons still shared the streets with cars, and you would always have to watch where you stepped when crossing the street.

Stevie was the barber's son from across the street. Irving was the son of the candy-store owner, Mr. Bialek. Around the corner on 153rd were Lenny and his younger brother Larry. We would spend most of our time together in the schoolyard of the Bronx High School of Science on 152nd street, which was a trade school for kids who weren't going on to college. It's where I learned to play handball, and stickball, and started becoming "Americanized".

Meeting my American Cousins—

About this time, my father and uncle Larry decided to go to Syracuse to visit my aunt Filomena, the sister that my father had arranged a marriage for. Aunt Clara's brother Phil borrowed a car, and we all piled in. Aunt Clara was from Syracuse, and her family was also there.
The ride was long and uncomfortable. There were no superhighways. When we finally got there, we parked in the driveway, and they sent me to ring the bell and ask if the Abbattista family lived there. Puzzled, I did as I was told, and when a lady answered the bell and opened the door, I politely asked, "Abita qui la famiglia Abbattista?" Imagine my surprise, when she yells out my name "Vitino", rushes out, and starts hugging and kissing me. How did she know who I was? What gave me away? I was flabbergasted, and obviously still not too bright!

We met my uncle Luigi, my older cousins Rose and Christine, and Carl, who was approximately my age. His real name was Aldino, but nobody called him that. They were all so totally different from anyone I had known before. As a matter of fact, Syracuse was totally different from anything I had ever experienced. Wide tree-lined streets, rich green grass, homes set on large pieces of property, with a separate garage, and a loft above the garage. The house had a covered porch, large rooms, and a big basement, with a washing machine! The parents spoke English, and ate foods I had never tried. I tasted my first Ritz cracker and jelly, cheeses that were not provolone, and fudge! In the basement, there were trunks full of clothing, and the cousins would play dress-up, and entertain the grownups. After dinner in the evenings, we would sit in the parlor, and the cousins would play. They had a regular piano, which Rose played, accompanied by Chris on her violin. Carl also played the violin, but he was still learning.

Carl had a collection of homemade wooden guns, all of which had strong rubber bands nailed to the front of the barrel. The bands could be pulled back, over the top, and fastened to the trigger area. Then you could slip a small square piece of linoleum in-between, and the gun was ready to fire! What fun, and the loft above the garage was his personal play room. His friends were so American-looking, with names like "Whitey", "Butch", "Rusty". He took me to the park, to play football with his friends. I didn't know how to play football, but the grass was so thick, it felt like I was falling on a mattress. Syracuse was a whole new world for me.

I don't remember the exact dates, but I know I spent time in Syracuse over the next few years, without my parents. The first time was in the summertime, because I remember going to Green Lake for a swim. Carl and I would spend all day together, and at night we would spread heavy blankets and cushions on the carpeted floor in the family room to sleep. At least that was the idea. We would spend most of the night talking or playing. On our knees, we would straddle our cushions, pull on the corner as the reins, and ride those imaginary horses after the bad guys, or chased each other, shooting imaginary guns. We would take breaks to sneak into the kitchen, and raid the oven, where the fudge was stored in its baking sheet. Tired of that, we would go out to the covered porch, open the front door, and take turns "mooning" the neighborhood. Of course, there was nobody roaming the streets at that time, but we thought we were being very courageous.

Our overactive imaginations finally caught up to us. One night, we heard the street door creak open into the enclosed patio. There was another door that protected us from the porch, and we went to the window to see who was visiting at this hour. We saw the street door was closed, but to the left, at a sharp angle, the rocking chair was rocking, and sitting in it was a black shape, with a round black hat (like Zorro's) on its head. We pulled back, and ran into the other room. It's possible I may have peed a little bit into my underwear. We thought about waking the adults, but decided to make sure we had seen what we had seen first. I don't know how long it took us to build up enough courage to take another look, but when we finally crept up to the inside window and looked out, the black shape was gone . . . but *the rocking chair was still rocking*!!! To this day, I will swear I saw what I saw, and so will Carl.

Eventually, we'd fall asleep, and wake up to a breakfast of cereal, bacon and eggs, toast and jelly, etc. To someone used to having "zuppa di latte", pieces of bread in sugared warm milk and coffee, this was really different. Even more amazing was going to the side door, lifting the lid on a metal container, and taking out bottles of milk! I accompanied Carl around the neighborhood while he sold subscriptions to The Saturday Evening Post, so as to earn the prize of a football. It was great.

I was also there in wintertime. Amazing! Woke up in the morning, to find snow up to my shoulders outside. After breakfast, it was our chore to clear a path. Everything was so pure white and undisturbed, it seemed a shame to ruin it by shoveling. After a while, I stopped seeing the beauty, because it stopped being fun, and started being work. By the time we cleared a path to the garage, I was ready to go back to the Bronx. Fortunately I stayed, and got to ride a sleigh and a toboggan. Spring Street had a slight incline, and was great for sleigh riding. The toboggan was another matter. We never got the hang of steering it, and it would go its own way. On one trip, Carl decided he was George Washington, and stood up with his foot on the curled-up front of the toboggan. We were going pretty fast, when we slammed into a snow bank, and Carl went flying off, bouncing off a tree headfirst, knocking himself out. He lay still for what seemed a long time, and I remember being truly panicked, not knowing what to do. Fortunately, he came to, and we never mentioned it to anyone, or even spoke about it to each other.

Another time, I was there long enough to attend school, sharing time in the same class as Carl. The people talked funny. They said "waaater" instead of "water", "albow" for "elbow", "ruf" for "roof", but otherwise were very open and friendly. This must have been a little later, because Carl had a girlfriend, which he wouldn't talk about. Just as well, because girls were something of which I knew absolutely nothing about! One of his friends told me that the family knew, but did not approve. He would find ways to go on errands without me, and we didn't spend as much time together as on previous visits. Nevertheless, I have only good memories of Syracuse, and my "American" cousins.

*   *   *

Back in the Bronx, I was coming along just fine. I had discovered comic books, which fit in perfectly with the alternate universe I tended to live in. You were either a Superman guy or a Batman guy, and I was a Batman guy. He was more real, he had Robin to worry about, and he had to work hard to get the job done, while Superman could fly, look through walls, and could lift anything. I was always happy when somebody zapped him with kryptonite. I didn't want him killed, just taught a lesson. Besides, I really liked the original Captain Marvel, where Billy Batson would holler "Shazam", be struck by lightning, and become the superhero! I loved all those early superheroes. The Torch, Green Lantern, Green Arrow, Daredevil, The Falcon, The Atom, The Shadow, Plastic Man, and with World War II joined by Wonder Woman, Captain America, and others. I waited for each new issue, and accumulated a lot of comic books. Obviously, nobody could afford to buy all the comic books, so trading was a big thing to catch up on all the missed ones. Besides, I would never spend my money to buy cartoon comics like Looney Tunes, but they were the first I would trade for. Here also we had to choose, and I was more of a Donald Duck guy than a Mickey Mouse guy, with the others right behind. I especially enjoyed Porky Pig and that "pesty wabbit."

The Japanese attack of Pearl Harbor on December 7, 1941 was a historic day, but I have no particular memory of it. I was aware of the war because it seemed all the movies had to do with it. There were drives to collect newspapers, tin cans, and to turn in used oil over to the local butcher shops for recycling (I guess). Later came ration books for meat, sugar, and probably gasoline (for which we had no use since we didn't have a car). There were Air Raid Wardens, and practice air raids, and practice blackouts (which were called brownouts because some small lights were allowed, if they weren't visible from the street). The Air Raid Wardens could give summonses for violations, or so we believed. However, we had no attacks, and it all really seemed like playing a game, especially since we really didn't have any family members in the war. Well, that may be technically correct, but not true. Aunt Clara's brother Phil was drafted, went through training, and his group was shipped out. Phil didn't show up at the ship, and deserted. He claimed to have found out that the ship carrying his buddies was sunk, but I don't know how he could have possibly known, and we never spoke about it. I do know that he was hiding out for the rest of his life, never able to participate at family gatherings, or behave like a normal citizen. The FBI regularly checked with aunt Clara by phone and in person for years and years afterward. I believe he made a living as a hot dog vendor, and wound up living with some woman because he couldn't get married

Before making friends with Stevie, Irving, and Lenny, I wandered into the PAL Recreation Center on 153rd Street and Morris Ave, which ran parallel to Courtland Ave. Kids were playing games, and it looked like fun. I also met a girl named Lucy, and was smitten. She showed me how to play some of the board games, but I really wasn't paying attention. The next day I went to the center, and saw her on the balconied second floor. She waved, and told me to come up. I went to the inside staircase, but never made it upstairs. At the first landing, I was met by three guys, one of whom informed me that Lucy was his girlfriend, and to make sure I understood, threw me down the stairs. Fortunately, only my pride was hurt. I understood, but I wasn't about to give up that easily. So, I started hanging out with the guys, and tried to become their friend, figuring that sooner or later Lucy would like me better. I very quickly found out that Morris Ave was not Courtland Ave. Some of these guys had already been left back in school at least once, and at least one of them had spent time in reform school. Plus, their idea of fun was scary. Once, I found them surrounding a cat that they had tied to the wall with a long rope. Each of them was holding a thin branch, which they would use to whip the cat, when it came their way. I found a reason to leave right away, hoping not to show how scared I was of them. They also told me they enjoyed dropping a cat into a barrel half full of water, and time how long it would take before it drowned. Their favorite though, was dowsing a cat with a flammable liquid, and setting it on fire. Then they would chase the torch, and watch it die. I realized I really didn't like Lucy that much anyway, and stayed on my own block.

There's a PS to this story. Years later (maybe 7 or 8), I was on the subway going to Manhattan, when we passed my old neighborhood stop of 149th Street. On board came Lucy. I recognized her immediately, and when she saw me, I know she recognized me also, but continued past me. She was dressed in a ratty make-believe fur jacket, big costume jewelry, short skirt, very high heels, and overly made-up. If she wasn't a prostitute, she sure looked like one. Funny thing though, I still saw the pretty Lucy from the PAL

I never shared my outside experiences at home. Like in Corato, my mother gave me a long leash, and I only confided in her when I was in trouble, or if I needed something. The routine of life at home picked up on the weekends, when there was no school, and I could sleep late. Mike was about four years old, and a really cute kid. He would come into my bedroom and wake me up, if I wasn't already awake. We would then play games, like the bed was a truck, and we had to drive through enemy territory, and he would shoot at the enemy soldiers while I drove . . . . or we would pull the bed sheet over the headboard, and play inside the "tent". His favorite though, was to play "Superman".

One side of my bed was pushed up against the wall. I would lay with my back on the bed, and my legs on the wall, with my feet towards the ceiling. Then, I would bend my knees, and bring my feet as far down as possible without leaving the wall. I would then sit Mike on the soles of my feet, and start pushing up towards the ceiling, with both of us yelling, "Up, up, and away!" When my legs were all straightened out, I would then push away from the wall, and Mike would "fly" down to the bed. We both enjoyed the game.

After meals at night, we would generally listen to an Italian station on the radio. Our favorite program was about an Italian family with a fat daughter named Rosa, who they were trying to marry off to Luigi. Every time he would come around, the father would say, "Rosa, say hello to Luigi". She would say, "Hello, Luigi", and giggle. He would then answer in an exasperated tone, "Hello, Rosa". This same routine was repeated every night; we waited for it, and laughed on queue every time.

If the weather permitted, we would sit on the terrace and people-watch. I would be sent to fill a bottle with seltzer from the fountain at the candy store, or maybe buy some ice cream. On warm summer nights I was sent across the street to get a quart of draft beer from the bar

Other times we would visit uncle Larry and aunt Clara, or we would go for a walk down on 3rd Avenue. We would window-shop the closed stores, and I would chase Mike around my parents while they walked. One time, he wasn't watching where he was running, and ran into an open metal cellar door. The edge caught him just below the eye, and it started bleeding. My parents yelled at me, but I was just thankful it didn't damage the eye. I never chased him again, and he carries the scar to this day.

Sometimes I would accompany my father to visit "the single guys", uncle Ralph, uncle Danny, and Phil (before he went into the Army). They shared an apartment on 149th Street, near Courtland Avenue. It had a big kitchen, and the bathtub was next to the kitchen sink. Fortunately, we never caught anybody in the tub when we visited.

Actually, uncle Ralph was married, but his wife was in Corato, and she couldn't get permission to enter the U.S.. I think she couldn't pass the physical exam. Whatever the reason, they never saw each other again after he left her. Maybe that was why he drank more wine than he should have. Uncle Ralph was a shoemaker, and uncle Larry had loaned him the money to set up his own shop on 149th Street. I understood that this was the second shop, because he had been losing money on the first one, and he wasn't doing so well with the second. The brothers believed this was due to his drinking habits, but I never saw him drunk. I thought he was the most dignified-looking of the brothers. My father would make fun of him, but never to his face, because he figured uncle Ralph had never lived up to his responsibilities as the oldest brother. He would occasionally visit us for Sunday dinner, but we otherwise saw very little of him. We saw a lot of uncle Larry and aunt Clara, and he was a big influence in my life. Although I'll be writing about him as I go along, this is probably a good time to formally introduce my "zio Lorenzo".

Lorenzo Sciancalepore (4/18/1908-6/10/1985)

Uncle Larry was the baby of the nine children, and maybe that was why his thinking was different from the others. He enjoyed a good laugh, even if it was at his own expense. When I had occasion to speak to his sisters in Italy, they would invariably laugh when remembering his childhood.

One story was of the time his big brother Ralph sent him to buy an after dinner cigar. He didn't come back for a long time, and when he did, he had no cigar, and no money. He pleaded to the whole family that it wasn't his fault. He was on the way to buy the cigar, when he passed a fruit store, and he saw the biggest cherries in the world. He couldn't move, and he couldn't take his eyes off the cherries. The next thing he knew, he had exchanged the cigar money for the cherries, and had eaten them all, before he realized what he had done. Ralph, deprived of his cigar, started to chase him, but Lorenzo ran to his father, and again pleaded as how it wasn't his fault. His father tried to be stern with him, pointing out that it wasn't his money to spend, but unfortunately, his father couldn't keep a straight face. Neither could the other brothers and sisters, and he got away with it.

As a boy, he had been apprenticed to learn how to make and repair wagon wheels, and he often joked about how he was lucky to be alive. It seems he had a hard time following orders, and would rather play than work. The "maestro" would get very angry, and throw his hammer at him. Uncle Larry said he never learned how to make wagon wheels, but he sure was good at dodging those hammers.

While the other brothers came to America legally, and their names are recorded at Ellis Island, Lorenzo sneaked in. In 1926 (18 years old), he paid to be smuggled in, and spent the Atlantic crossing hidden in the cargo hold of the ship. The waiters brought him food, and when the ship docked, he walked off with the waiters. He later went to Canada, and reentered legally, so as to get his citizenship.

He was as hard a worker as my father, but he wasn't afraid to go on his own. While my father looked to be paid for his day's work, uncle Larry figured he could make more money if he worked for himself. He didn't have much money, so the choices were few, and that's how he got to be an iceman.

When I first met him in 1940, he was an iceman. He said that he had started carrying ice the year I was born. He had a route in Harlem, which he used to walk to every day, taking 149th Street until he crossed the bridge into Harlem. I visited him a few times, and got a feel for the work he did. His "route" was a couple of blocks of apartment houses, none more than six floors, and no elevators. He had a pushcart with a few "kegs" of ice, about one foot square, and five foot long. There were no refrigerators. They were called iceboxes. The piece of ice would go in the top, same as the refrigerator freezer, and the coolness would be transmitted to the food stored below.

He would buy the ice from a truck that would come around a couple of times a day, and store some of it in a basement he rented. The rest would be in the pushcart, covered by a few burlap sacks (to delay melting). Although he knew who needed what on any given day, he was always getting called for extra deliveries. It was a sight to see black women, hanging out of windows, yelling, "Hey Tony, I want a 25-cent piece today". The price range would be from 10 to 25 cents. He would take their orders from the street, and joke or barter with them, trying to get them to buy a bigger piece of ice. Then he would make comments to me about each one of them, like the one who would always give him a tip, or the one that wanted a 25-cent piece for 10 cents, or the one who had gone to another iceman, and now wanted to come back. He would then cut a chunk of ice with his ice pick, put it into a small wooden tub, place the tub on his shoulder (cushioned by a sack), and walk up from two to six flights of stairs to make the deliveries, <u>one at a time</u>.

He worked long hours for six and a half days a week (he took off Sunday afternoons), and was very proud of the fact that he had worked right through the Depression. He set up his brother Donato (Danny), as well as Phil, but neither of them did anywhere near as well as uncle Larry. Besides being very hard work, it was also potentially very dangerous. He was a white man in a black world, and all alone. He was held up a number of times while coming down from a delivery, but was never mugged. It says something for his character. He told me that on those occasions, he didn't object to giving over the money, because he knew he could earn more money. However, he made it very clear that if they wanted to hurt him, then they were going to have to "talk to my ice pick".

Eventually, he got a driver's license, and an ice truck, and life got a little easier. But when the refrigerators came, he was out of business. It didn't happen all at once, so he saw it coming, and had a chance to sell his route.

After a period of working at odd jobs, he decided to get back into business, and bought a bar in the Bronx. The neighborhood was multiracial, and tougher than Harlem, because by this time, drugs had started to appear on the scene. The area was depicted in a movie called "Fort

Apache" with Paul Newman. Because of this, and because he liked to watch western movies, I used to kiddingly call him "The Sheriff of Freeman Street". He bought a second bar in the area, in partnership with his brother Donato, which brought him nothing but headaches, because of his brother. For example, if a fight broke out in the bar, uncle Danny would go hide in the bathroom until it was over. Considering you could lose your liquor license if you got a summons for fighting on the premises, this was not a bright thing to do.

Another time, uncle Danny went to the local Police precinct, and in public, told the officers on duty to "take better care of my bar", reminding one and all that he was "paying for their protection". Very embarrassing for all concerned, and uncle Larry was told to keep his brother hidden, if he knew what was good for him.

Another time, when uncle Danny found out that the bartenders were stealing bottles of liquor, his solution was to steal more than the bartenders. When he proudly told uncle Larry what he had done, and showed off his stash of stolen bottles, uncle Larry couldn't believe it. However, instead of ranting and raving, he pointed out to his brother that he was only stealing from himself. Apparently, this had not occurred to uncle Danny. I think you get the picture.

It was uncle Larry who bought the house on 243rd Street, and moved us all "uptown". He turned it into a two-family dwelling, and we rented and lived together for almost forty years, until after my father died.

When we came back from Italy in 1957, uncle Larry gave me a job managing his bar on week-ends, which allowed me to go to NYU full-time, to study engineering. A few years later, he loaned Mike and I the money so we could buy our first newspaper delivery business.

I'll talk more about uncle Larry as I go along, but he was another one of the people who had a bearing on my life. He loved his family, worked hard, wasn't afraid to take chances, and always enjoyed a good laugh, even if it was at his own expense. A couple that come to mind are:

As an iceman, he had discovered the importance of "dressing in layers" long before it became fashionable. This allowed him to be ready for any weather, and he was rarely sick. Especially in the winter, when he came home, and started peeling off his clothing like onionskin, it was a sight to watch the mound of clothing accumulate. My father would kid him unmercifully, and uncle Larry would just nod, and laugh with him.

He also was a big believer in sweating out an illness. On those rare occasions when he didn't feel well, he would put some extra clothing on top of his flannel underwear, have hot tea and whiskey, go to bed covered with extra blankets, and sweat all night. Invariably, the next morning, all would be well. A hot bath, an alcohol rubdown, and he was set to go.

His "chicken" story, and "c'mere dahly" story go along with my "Mikey" stories as my favorites, and you can read them there. Judge for yourself.

*   *   *

Now, back to my life as a twelve-year-old. Having learned the language, and with friends, I became rather full of myself. With all the movies that I saw, I became convinced I could be a movie star. My mother of course agreed, and provided me with a picture that I promptly sent off to the movie studios, together with a note explaining how I was also bilingual. I actually got a letter back from one of the studios (I think it was 20th Century Fox), saying they didn't have anything for me now, but would keep my name on file.

I also continued to try to get a girlfriend. I had no idea what to do with a girlfriend, but it was great to say you had one. After striking out with Lucy, I found out that the baker's daughter across the street had just broken up with her "boyfriend". Actually, he was the one who told me, and warned me that she would make me get rid of my friends, just to prove that I liked her. Being forewarned, I was ready when she began to ask me not to hang out with Steve and Irving. When I told her I wouldn't do it, she kicked me. I promptly kicked her back harder, and that was the end of the affair. Such is the way of young love.

About this time I also picked up a couple of bad habits. Just sitting around, with nothing to do, Steve and I developed a game. If we saw pretty women coming, we would start wrestling on the ground, rolling into their legs. This allowed us to look up their dresses. I don't know what we expected to see. Honestly, in all the times we did it, I may have seen a knee once, and that was probably my imagination.

Also, I learned how to hitch on the outside of a trolley car. A wheel that rolled on an overhead electrical line powered the trolley. When the trolley reached the end of the line, the seats would be reversed, the conductor would go to the other end where there were duplicate sets of controls, and the trolley would reverse its course. The front rod would be pulled down, and the rear rod would be connected to the overhead power line. Pulling or releasing the rope connected to the rod did this. The rope was stored in a spool outside the trolley on both ends. This was the prime holding place when hitchhiking. It was fun. We kids would wait until the trolley got started, then run and ride on the back of the trolley. When it stopped to pick up or drop off passengers, we would make sure to get off and get back a respectful distance, because it wasn't unusual for the conductor to chase us. Sometimes, the conductor had an assistant on board, and those were much harder to ride. I didn't know any of the kids I rode with. I don't remember why I started, but I can't blame it on any of my friends.

About this time, my mother decided I should learn to play the piano. She set me up with a teacher for weekly lessons, and since we had no room for a piano, I would go to his studio. My mother gave me two dollars for the lesson, and change for the trolley. I saved the change by hitchhiking. After a few weeks, I realized that I wasn't learning anything, and it seemed such a waste of two dollars. So, I enjoyed the ride, but I skipped the lessons, and kept the money to buy comic books. The scam came to a screeching halt when one of the neighbors saw me on the back of a trolley car, and reported it to my mother. She threatened to tell my father, and I promised I would never do it again, and I didn't.

However, there was no shortage of things I could get in trouble for. As I said before, this was wartime, and we would have practice blackout drills, to prepare for air raids that never came. Steve and I found this to be a fun time, with no cars moving, and everything quiet. We would go in the back yards, jump the fences between properties, and peek in the back windows of neighbors' houses. One time, we were having so much fun, we didn't realize how late it was until we heard Steve's father, the barber, yelling for him. He was getting it good when I left him, and found my parents in an equally angry mood. My father really yelled at me, and sent me to bed without dinner. However, he wasn't finished. I could hear him telling my mother how angry I made him. He kept getting louder and louder, angrier and angrier, until he couldn't take it anymore. Then, he would jump out of his chair, come into my bedroom, and beat on me. This would calm him down, and he would return to the kitchen table. Unfortunately, he would start working himself up all over again, and the process would repeat itself a number of times. Even more unfortunately, and for the first time ever, my mother also got very angry, and she also started taking turns at me. I had never been physically disciplined before, but I realized I more than deserved it.

Let me be quick to point out that I had no broken bones, no black and blue marks, and it really didn't hurt. As a matter of fact, when they were beating on me, I wondered why it didn't hurt. I mean, they screamed while they were hitting me, and I yelled with every blow, but there was no damage done. Even then, I realized their anger was because they were concerned.

Steve's father blamed me as the bad influence, and my father was certain it was "the barber's son". In any case, Steve and I did not pal around any more after that day.

I wish I could say that school was going well, but it wouldn't be true. I really don't know what I was doing wrong, but the teacher didn't like me. Maybe it was because we sat in alphabetical order, and my desk was in the back of the class. This maybe made me not pay attention, which then made me talk with the other kids, especially the girls, when I wasn't supposed to. I said maybe. I know for sure that she didn't like it when I jabbed the kid sitting in front of me in his rear end with the sharp end of my compass. That's why I was very happy to be finished with fifth grade.

Unfortunately, when I reported to start the sixth grade, I found the same teacher. She went to great lengths to assure us that this was a fresh start, and the "blackboard has been erased". Obviously, she wasn't talking to me, because at the first opportunity, she accused me of "picking up where I had left off" the year before. She would take me outside class, and into the stairwell, where she would yell at me for the smallest things. It was clear I had gotten under her skin, and I also didn't like her. After a few months, I finally told my mother. As usual, she came to my defense. At the end of the semester, she took me out of public school, and enrolled me in Catholic School, Our Lady of Pity on 151st Street.

Catholic School-a change of life experience

Public Schools divided the school year into two semesters, A and B, while Catholic Schools did not. The curriculums also were not the same. Since I transferred in mid-year, I missed out on things covered in the first half, and not taught in Public School in the same period. The most notable, and something I've had trouble with my whole life, was the diagramming of sentences. Beyond identifying a noun or a pronoun, the rest was a jungle. Verbs, adjectives, etc., have always been mysteries to me. Fortunately, I've always had a knack for using the right word, and what I lost on the technical side, I made up in spelling and composition.

Another big change was the nuns! They were so sweet and understanding when my mother brought me to be enrolled. When my mother left me with my new 6th grade teacher, she asked me if I had already had breakfast, and brought me a tray with milk and cookies. Even my mother didn't do that, unless I was sick! I thought, "What a great move. Why didn't we do this before?" For the first few weeks, she was very solicitous; going over my homework with me, pointing out my mistakes, praising every little good thing I did. She always made sure I had understood the material covered in class, and always asked me if she was going too fast. I always reassured her that I could keep up.

I felt privileged to be treated this way. Especially since I noticed she wasn't all that nice to the other kids! I didn't care. For the first time in my life, I loved going to school. I even started to study a little at home, so that I could be complimented the next day. I started to look forward to my daily dose of being patted on the back. I quickly realized it had to be because I was so much smarter than the rest of the class, and it should be the teacher who should feel privileged to have me in her class.

The change was so subtle that I didn't realize it until it was too late! The compliments came less often, and less lavish. There always seemed to be something wrong with my homework, and I started to be called on more and more in class. Before my eyes, that very sweet lady turned into a habit-wearing very demanding monster! I still sat in the back of the room, but it seemed like I was the only one in the class. If I even began to turn around in my seat, she scolded me. If my eyes wandered from my desk during an assignment, she scolded me. If I spoke out-of-turn, or if I didn't respond promptly to questions, she scolded me. It always seemed she called on me when I didn't know the answer. I also had a hard time knowing where she was all the time. If I started daydreaming, I would get a shot in the back of the head. She moved so fast! One second she was in the front of the class, the next she was bouncing the back of the blackboard eraser off my head. I'm sure my classmates enjoyed it, but they couldn't show it. Otherwise, they would get it worse. It was a marvel to see her move, when I wasn't the victim. She zipped between rows of desks without effort, seemingly on rollers. The forward movement would raise the sides of her cowl, giving the illusion of two miniature airplane wings, which helped her fly.

Being the smart guy that I was, I quickly figured out her game plan. So, I started double-checking my homework, to make sure I understood it, because I knew I would be called the next morning. Also, I started paying attention to every word she said, and when she tried to catch me unaware, I was ready. I could almost see the disappointment in her face when I gave the correct answer. Little by little, she called on me less and less, and soon it was like I didn't even exist. She was too busy torturing other souls, and I really enjoyed the spectacle, but made sure not to show it. I was very smug about how I had beaten her.

She accomplished more in a couple of months than all the combined teachers had done in the previous seven years. I even began enjoying going to school. I long ago forgot her real name, because in my mind I will always remember her as Sister Potato-face.

Sister Potato-face knew she was going to lose me to the 7th grade, so she devised one last act to further oppress me. She volunteered my services as an altar boy, and told me to report to the Parish Pastor. He had such a bad personality, I was sure he must have been her real father. Except he was bad from the very first day! No patience, incomplete instructions, very demanding, and expected that I should speak and understand Latin as if it was my native tongue. It didn't help that I figured he must be a drunk. How else could you explain the fact that, when I brought the wine and water to him during the mass, he would take all the wine, but woe if I poured more than one drop of water into the chalice. He would grunt, and give me the dirtiest look.

Fortunately, the assistant Pastor was the total opposite. Father Gregory always had a smile, was very patient, and kept repeating instructions in a friendly way, until we got it right. This was critical for me when serving a Solemn High Mass, which is offered by at least three priests, and a number of altar boys. In over two years, I never got the hang of it, and never knew where to stand or what to do. Fortunately, Father Gregory was always there, to nod me into the right direction, or whisper instructions. He was as positive as the Pastor was negative. He also rewarded the altar boys with occasional day trips, like taking us all to Coney Island.

Once again, my life changed. It was tough, but I enjoyed Catholic school, and I especially enjoyed being an altar boy. So much so, that I volunteered to serve the daily 6 AM Mass. My mother would wake me, and I would walk to Church. After Mass, I would come home, have a breakfast, and return to school with Mike for classes. Sometimes, I would be called from class to serve a special Mass, and I felt like such a big shot! Especially once when Archbishop Spellman came to visit (before he was elevated to Cardinal).

My family was not church going, except for Palm Sunday. My father didn't want to be caught without palms to exchange, when offered by others. My mother was religious, but not of the regular church going variety. This left me on my own, as usual, and I was fine with it. I enjoyed going to serve Mass in the early morning hours, and walking the dark deserted streets gave me a special connection to God, and I felt privileged. So much so, that on those cold winter mornings, I would collect stray cats on the way, and bring them into the Church vestibule to warm up. After all, the Franciscan Fathers ran the Our Lady of Pity Church, and St. Francis was the patron Saint of animals, wasn't he? I felt I was doing God's work. Nobody ever caught me doing it, but I had a sneaking suspicion that the Pastor would not approve. Probably not even Father Gregory.

I even brought a cat home. It was a cold winter day, I was playing outside the house, and I saw a little kitten under a parked car, looking for something to eat. I got a little saucer of milk, and little by little, got him to come inside from the cold, and then brought him upstairs. My mother gave me a dime, and I went across the street to the butcher, to get some liver for the cat. My mother wasn't hard to convince, and I had my first pet. A black cat, with white paws, and a white nose. I had just finished reading the fairy tale "Puss in Boots", and I named him "Boots", because it looked like he was wearing white boots. I never really knew if it was a boy or a girl, but I suspect it was a boy because it spent a lot of time outside and never got pregnant. I talked to Boots a lot, and he would sit and look at me all the while. I was positive he understood what I was saying, and I made sure that he ate well.

The seventh grade was a continuation of the sixth, except it was tougher, and so was the teacher. While potato-face would use the back of the blackboard eraser, this new one had a personal pointer, which had many uses. She would use it as an extension of her finger, when pointing to someone. She would use it to review work on the blackboard. She would use it as a baton, to emphasize a particular point she wanted to make, or to tap you on the head, if she felt that your brains needed a little unscrambling. Even when she let it rest in the center of her desk, it was in plain sight, and served as a reminder to the class. It was red, about a foot long and 1-2 inches wide. It may have been cut from the top of a broomstick. I became personally acquainted with it on several occasions. One occasion was more personal than others. Sister would call students to the blackboard, to demonstrate the math problems assigned for homework from the day before. She used the same technique as potato-face, calling on those who didn't do it right the first time, until they mended their ways. I had started to backslide, and was not doing my homework as religiously as before. As a result, I was being called to the blackboard almost every day. Invariably, I would be doing it wrong, and she would stop me, and point out my errors, using the pointer as emphasis. Apparently, she wasn't getting through to me. So one day, as I was writing, chalk in hand, I once again made a mistake. This time the pointer came down, and nailed my hand to the blackboard, squashing it like a spider! After school, my hand started to swell, and my mother took me to the doctor. He wrapped my hand in bandages, and I was excused from homework for two weeks. I was so happy, because I figured I got the best of the deal, and boy, did I show her! However, I once again became very attentive in class, and made sure my homework was the best I could do. What did my parents have to say about this? Well, if she hit me, I must have deserved it, and if I didn't straighten up, I would get the rest from them!

While I was getting religion on one side, I hadn't really totally converted. That other side was still making me do things. Some were OK, like sending away for the Charles Atlas muscle building equipment, so that I could become a muscle man, instead of a "95 pound weakling". This was one of the ads on the back of the comic books I was addicted to. There was also the "Red Ryder B-B Gun". I think it only cost something like $2.50, and I got permission to order it. While I never became a muscle man, I did get to be pretty good with the b-b gun.

At first, I put a glass gallon container on top of a crate, and placed it in the back yard. I would then shoot at it from the kitchen window. Eventually, I would hit it so many times, that the container would fall apart. Then I would get another container, and place it back farther. When I ran out of yard, I started using smaller targets. Eventually, it started to get boring, and I started to look for new challenges.

Irving had a younger brother named Albie, and they both had to shovel the sidewalk in front of their candy store after a snowstorm. I was watching them one day, noticing that Albie was such a chubby kid, and what a big rear end he had when he bent over to shovel. I wondered if I could hit him in his fat rear, from my distance of a half a block away, using my trusty Red Ryder b-b gun. From thought to deed, I called Steve over (this was before the air raid episode), and he acted as decoy. He stood in front of my doorway. I cracked it open enough to put the muzzle of the b-b gun out, and the next time Albie bent over, I shot him. He yelled, jumped up, and started rubbing his backside. He looked around, but had no clue as to why he had just gotten this pain. Irving figured he was trying to get out of shoveling, so he yelled at him. When Albie bent down again, I got him again. Again the same routine. When I hit him a third time, Albie had had enough! He dropped everything, and went inside, leaving his brother with a puzzled look on his face. When Irving would look our way, Steve was looking elsewhere, and I was out of sight. It was really, really funny.

Sometime after that, I was on my front terrace with my b-b gun, when I saw Steve coming. He was about a block away. I raised my rifle, brought him into my sights, and yelled "Bam-Bam". He saw me, and picked up on the game. Raising his arm, and pointing his forefinger at me, he yelled "Bam-Bam" back. Then he started to run towards me and we "Bam-Bammed" each other. Then he started to zigzag as he ran, and the challenge was too much for my trigger finger. I really really didn't expect to hit him, and I was shocked when I saw him grab his left arm. The shock on my face was matched by the shock on his. He ran upstairs to where I was, yelling and asking how I could do such a stupid thing. All I could say was that I hit him by mistake, but realized it could have been serious. I was so relieved that he didn't tell his father or my parents, and never shot at anyone thereafter.

That doesn't mean I stopped using my b-b gun. I figured the area between 153-154 Streets was "my area", and needed my protection. So, I proceeded to place a b-b hole in every plate glass store window that fronted my apartment. I placed it in the corner, so it wouldn't be an eyesore, but it was my signature. I was very proud of my accomplishment. Of course, I couldn't share my secret with anyone, except Steve. In exchange, I didn't signature his barbershop. This would confirm that, on some level, I knew it was wrong!

The 8th grade brought also the meeting of my next great love, Marie Rapetti. It also had the villain, Frank Iamarino. They knew each other before I got there, and he would taunt me about how she liked him better than me. Besides that, his grades were always a little better than mine. As a matter of fact, at our elementary school graduation ceremony, I was awarded the math medal, but Frank got the general excellence medal. Eight of the boys took the entrance exam to Cardinal Hayes High School, and four passed. I was the second to be accepted, but Frank was the first. We didn't share any classes in high school, but he continued to haunt me. We both chose to play in the school band, and we both chose to play the clarinet. However, I played 3rd clarinet badly, and was a substitute player at the football games, without my own uniform, while Frank was 1st clarinet, and was so good that he played on the high school swing band. I consoled myself with the fact that I was also on the handball team, and on the track team, and he was short! From the high school alumni newspaper, I learned that Frank went on to have a career with IBM, had three children, and retired while I was having this roller-coaster ride of a life. However, I'm sure he never got any taller!

Anyway, back to grammar school, and Marie Rapetti. She lived just around the corner from me on 153rd Street, and I got into the habit of hanging out with her in front of her house after dinner. I'm sure she liked me after school, but she liked Frank better during school, and would go walking with him during lunch, and he would make faces at me behind her back. No, I never hit him. Of course, this would make me want to make the most of my opportunities when I had her undivided attention after school. I would take Mike along with me, and meet Marie and her girlfriend in front of her house, and talk or play ball. On one of these occasions, the ball bounced into her side-yard, which was surrounded by a tall iron picket fence. I saw my opportunity to impress her, so I quickly climbed the fence, jumped over, and retrieved the ball. The smile she gave me lit up the sky, and I could have floated up and over the fence on the way back. Unfortunately, I had to climb it again, and it didn't go so well. Feeling so wonderful, I wasn't careful. I lost my hold, and as I slipped off, the pointed pike gashed the palm of my left hand. Instantly, I knew it was serious. I didn't want to look at it, so I made a fist, excused myself, and headed for home. Mike kept jumping up and down, wanting to see the damage. When we got far enough away from the girls, we took a peek, and saw a big gash, with a handful of blood. Mike stopped jumping up and down, and didn't say another word. My mother took me to the hospital, and I got about eight stitches. I can still see the scar.

I felt like such a jerk, and I didn't hang out by Marie any more. It was just as well, since we were graduating, and we wound up moving away shortly thereafter. Marie was also moving away. Another lost love!

1945 Graduation   me   Marie—front row   Frank
                                    (next to Pastor)   (last on right)

Other memories from this period: Mike coming to watch me serve Mass, and sitting in the front row. At the end of the Mass, as we were leaving the altar, Mike jumps up and starts clapping his hands, as if he had just witnessed a great show. Really cute!

I actually got paid to be in a real show. My mother was working part-time sewing new leather gloves for Mr. Liscio, who also worked as an actor on the Italian stage. One time he offered Steve and I a job on the stage, and he took us to the Brooklyn Music Hall, where he was performing in an Italian drama. What an experience! We were supposed to be underground revolutionaries, and had two brief appearances. In the first, we were sitting, listening to our leader making an impassioned speech, at the end of which we were to jump up and yell our approval. It was stressed that we had to watch for the signal from our group leader sitting at the end of the bench, and to get up only when he did. The makeup man put a mustache and sideburns on me, together with a hat, and I got a seat at the front of the stage, nearest the audience. I really wanted to make a good impression, but I had no idea how long the speech would last. So, I kept my eye on our group leader. When the talking stopped, and he began to move as if to get up, I jumped up and started yelling with as much enthusiasm as I could muster. Unfortunately, I had reacted so quickly, that I was the only one standing and yelling. Unlike making a movie, you only get one shot on stage! For the second showing, I had no makeup man, no mustache, and my seat was so far back on the stage, I could have been in my jockey shorts, and no one would have noticed. Now you would think this would have discouraged us. Not at all! It was fun watching the actors bustle around. Plus, there was a scene where a dancer did the "dance of the seven veils", and we would sneak a peek in her dressing room while she was putting on the veils for the dance. Great stuff for fourteen-year-old kids. Plus, we got paid $20 each, but no encore.

Another memory is my second and third fight, which came one after the other. Somehow, I had gotten into an argument with Carlo, a kid much bigger than me, but a little slow. Nobody messed with Carlo, so kids gathered to watch him beat me up. Instead of fighting with him, I wrestled, jumped on his back, and put a stranglehold on his neck. I was scared pickles of what he was going to do to me when he got me off his back, so I squeezed his neck as hard as I could. To my surprise, he raised his arms to show that he gave up, and I let him go. The other kids thought I was a big deal, and so did I. All except Lenny, who pointed out that I hadn't really fought the guy, and challenged me to take him on. Full of myself, and having just beaten a much bigger kid, I figured Lenny would be easy, considering I was a little bigger than he was. It was over in 30 seconds. He punched me in the nose, and in both eyes, and I realized how lucky I had been with Carlo. This time I raised my arms. Fortunately, the other kids had gone away, and the loss was only a private affair between Lenny and I.

I also had a job briefly as an errand boy in Jewish Deli. I would deliver groceries to customers' apartments, and restock shelves. I was amazed at how people could lie. It was wartime, and although sugar was rationed, it wasn't always available. So, while I was filling the shelves under the counter with one-pound bags of sugar, the boss would be telling some customer that he was still waiting for his next shipment of sugar. Of course, he was not talking to a regular customer, and he was saving his stock for the "regulars", but a lie is a lie, and I was amazed at how convincing he was while I was at his knees with a load of sugar! I got the job partly because my parents had bought me a bicycle, a beautiful black and white bike with fat tires. It had a horse emblem on the front steering column, and I named it "Black Beauty". We explored together. I even talked Irving and Lenny to take their bikes, and we went all the way to what would become LaGuardia airport. I can't tell you how far it was, but we left around 9 AM, and got back home around 5 PM. It was a Sunday, and our folks never knew where we had been.

I liked my neighborhood. I had learned to play handball and stickball, and even if I didn't have a lot of friends, I had no enemies. One of the few times I was uncomfortable was when my cousin Carl came to visit us from Syracuse. I told you how impressed I was with their place, and the Bronx just didn't measure up. Carl brought his brand new first-baseman baseball glove, and I arranged to get some guys together for a little baseball game. Unfortunately, the only playing field we had close by was an empty lot full of pebbles. We drew out a field, got a couple of bats from someplace, and a baseball that had long ago lost its original leather cover. It was almost an art form to know how to cover the threaded ball with a new cover of cloth adhesive tape. Carl never said anything, but we both knew Syracuse was another world. He only visited once.

Another uncomfortable moment was the day I graduated from Our Lady of Pity. After the ceremony at the Church, we all came back to our apartment, where uncle Larry and my father promptly got out of their jackets and ties, and we all sat down to have dinner together. In the middle of dinner, I hear my name being called from outside. Going out on the terrace, I see a bunch of my classmates, still all dressed up, downstairs in the street. They were visiting the homes of the graduating students, where parties were going on. I had no idea they knew where I lived, and I couldn't invite them up to meet my father and uncle Larry, sitting in their undershirt in front of a plate of macaroni. I made some excuse, got my jacket, and joined them on their rounds. What an eye-opener for me! We must have visited six or seven apartments, and there was a party in each one. People all dressed up, doors wide open for anyone to come in, us kids all being welcomed like royalty. We had sodas, sandwiches, candy, and other kinds of stuff I had never seen before. Then we would go to the next place, and the same thing all over again. After about three hours, I came back home to find my father and uncle Larry playing cards, and my mother and aunt Clara carrying on a regular conversation. I wasn't a big deal in my own house, and

I was struck by the difference. I knew it wasn't a lack of caring, but that they just didn't know any other way.

There is one last impression worth retelling about this period. Our landlord Eugenia and her husband lived behind the vegetable store below us, even though they owned the building, as well as the one next door. They had the apartments rented, and must have been doing all right, even though their lifestyle didn't show it. Anyway, Eugenia's husband died, and as was the custom, he was laid out on his bed for a day. My mother and I went downstairs to pay our respects, and sat in the few chairs set in a semicircle at the foot of the bed. One of the other renters saw the doors open, and walked in. We called her "la pazza", for obvious reasons. She wasn't bad enough to be committed, but wasn't always in touch with reality. Her uncared-for white hair sticking up in the air didn't help her image, but she lived by herself and was self-sufficient. Anyway, she took in the scene, but couldn't quite figure out what was going on. So, she walked around the bed, went up to the corpse, and put a hand on his forehead. Then, she turned to us, and with a solemn look, said, "You better call the doctor. I think he's got fever!" Having made the diagnosis, she promptly left. It wasn't the proper thing to do, but we couldn't help laughing. Even Eugenia, in her grief, couldn't help a little twitch of her lips.

We move Uptown

About this time, uncle Larry found out that our neighborhood was in for a dramatic change. Buildings were going to be torn down, and replaced by a Public Housing Project. The "Projects" didn't enjoy a good reputation, and uncle Larry didn't want to bring up his daughter in that environment. So, as was his style, he decided to move to a better neighborhood "uptown", and in no time at all, had bought a house on 243rd Street, on the Mount Vernon border. I knew nothing about all this until it was a done deal, and went up to see the house with my parents. It was a two-story one-family house, and my father agreed to convert it to a two-family home (at uncle Larry's expense), so we could live together. He knocked down some walls, and put up others, so that a kitchen and bathroom could be added upstairs, which would be our apartment.

As I said, I knew nothing about all this. One moment I was making sure that all the store windows had my "signature" b-b hole in the upper right-hand corner, the next I'm moving to another world. This change was almost as dramatic as when we arrived from Italy!

On the day of the move, while the men (my father, uncle Larry, and Phil) were loading what little furniture we had on uncle Larry's ice truck, my mother and I took the trolley to the new house. I lined an empty peach basket with newspapers, put Boots in it, and covered it. He wasn't too happy about the move, and proceeded to meow and crap until he was released. My first impression of the new neighborhood wasn't very good. After we got off the trolley, and were walking up 243rd Street, I saw a big kid (later found out it was Sonny Savitta) carrying a little rubber-tipped bow and arrow, chasing a little kid up the street, threatening to shoot him. I wondered, "What kind of "faggy" place is this?"

Actually, it was a very nice place. The street was lined with trees, and not that many buildings, although we had one across from us. It wasn't Syracuse, but it was much better than 153rd Street. There just seemed to be more space, and the kids weren't wise-ass. As a matter of fact, in the first couple of days after arriving, the doorbell rang, and a kid named Joey Amato introduced himself, and took me with him to meet the rest of guys "down the block". In time, my closest friends were Roddy Rowan (who lived in the building across the street from me), and Richie Schultz (who lived in the building down the block). I learned how to play box-ball, punch-ball, johny-on-the-pony, three-steps-to-Germany, kick-the-can, etc. All games that would keep us entertained without leaving the neighborhood. Also started playing baseball on a real field, with proper equipment. We would walk a mile up to Yonkers PS 11, but it was worth it. I had found another world.

My High School years:

In September of '45 I started attending Cardinal Hayes High School, which was now a 35-minute train ride away. I could have switched to a local high school, but I had committed to Hayes, and had passed a test that allowed me to attend the main school from the very first year (many students had to go to an annex for the first year). I was very proud to be a Hayes student, and still am. Hayes and 243rd Street helped reshape my character over the next four years, but not without a fight.

Cardinal Hayes' teachers were all brothers and priests, no nuns! This was a new experience for me. Well, at least since Professore Cinone in Corato. We were treated more like adults than kids, and were expected to behave as such. Unfortunately, high school freshmen are still really kids, and given the opportunity, will misbehave terribly. Even more unfortunately, I tended to misbehave more than most, given the opportunity.

My homeroom teacher Brother Brennan, and Father Pavis were very positive role models, and knew how to handle us without appearing to. Father Grace was another matter. An English teacher, and obviously very learned, he had no clue. He was OK with seniors, but shouldn't have been allowed to teach low-life freshmen. We started slowly, but with each success were challenged to see how far we could go. He accepted any excuse for missed homework, and always gave a second chance. Then, when his back was turned to face the blackboard, his notes would disappear from his desk, and his look of puzzlement at the loss was something to behold. He wasn't sure if someone had taken them, or if he had forgotten to take them out of his briefcase. Someone in the back of the room would then volunteer to have found them on the floor there, and he would become even more puzzled. When he was really confused, he would reach up with his right arm, over the top of his head, and scratch the left side of his face. This was the goal we set for ourselves for each class! Things such as throwing books into the wastebasket when his back was turned, just to see him jump from the sudden noise, went without punishment. Once he caught a student in the act, and contrary to his nature, went over and slapped him. The student overreacted, and went flying out of his seat and unto the floor. Father Grace wasn't aware he had hit him that hard, and was a little upset for the rest of the period. Imagine his surprise the next day, when the student showed up with his head all bandaged up, telling Father Grace it was the result of the previous days' "beating". This, though, was a little too much! He was sent to the school nurse for evaluation, was suspended for a few days, and spent the rest of the year in after-school detention (known as "jug").

For your information, I was not that student! Although, I did perform one act that would have gotten me expelled, had I been caught! Father Grace would keep the most troublesome boys sitting in the front row, where he could keep an eye on them. This didn't stop them from misbehaving, and he caught one of them in the act of shooting a water gun at him. That did it! He went to slap him, and had his left hand outstretched (palm down) for leverage. I was sitting in the back row, and had just finished eating a banana on the sneak. I don't know why, but I threw the banana peel up in the air, in the general direction of Father Grace. Watching it fly was like extra-slow-motion, and it was a one-in-a-million-shot. The banana peel landed on Father Grace's extended left hand, and stayed there, with two ends hanging off the index finger, and two from the pinky side. Father Grace looked at the banana skin, and for the life of him couldn't figure out how it had gotten there. He forgot about slapping the boy, reached up with his right arm, bent it over his head, and proceeded to scratch the left side of his face. The class was in an uproar, and totally out of control. We all got "jug", and nobody ever knew who threw the banana peel.

We knew we were being cruel, but just couldn't resist the opportunities. One was especially cruel, and was never repeated. We were told that Father Grace had a brother who had been in the paratroopers, and was recovering in a mental institution. Before class, someone drew a picture on the blackboard, of a figure coming down in a parachute, and printed HA-HA-HA-HA-HA coming from it. Father Grace silently erased it, and proceeded with the class as if nothing had happened. It was the only time he made us feel really ashamed of ourselves.

As you may imagine, not everyone was doing well in English, and many were looking forward to summer school, to make up for a failing grade. By this time, things had degenerated pretty badly, to the point that desks were put against the door, so Father Grace had to push his way into the classroom to begin the class. After the finals had been graded, and the tests returned, someone in another class stole the grade book from his briefcase, and passed it around. Many chose to improve their grades, and the book was returned to his briefcase before the end of the day. Unfortunately, some had gone back and reimproved their grade, to the point that it became noticeable the grade book had been tampered with. True to his nature, Father Grace didn't fail anyone, and never complained to the Dean of Discipline. The Dean would speak to us about proper behavior, as would our other teachers in reference to Father Grace, but we couldn't help ourselves, and "The Devil made me do it". Truth to tell, I had Father Grace again in junior year, and there were no incidents at all. He was a very good person, and I'm sorry for my behavior, but it sure was fun at the time. By the way, I didn't alter my grade. I think I had an honest B, and left it alone.

My second year brought me in contact with Father Jablonski, and we were to go head-to-head for the next three years. He was tall, with slicked back dark hair, and had a habit of wearing his cape over his shoulders, and was given the nickname of "Dracula". He was my Latin II teacher, and took no nonsense. I didn't like Latin, but needed at least two years, or I would have to take up another language. I struggled for the year, and was on the fail-pass border most of the time. I improved my homework grades by buying a copy of the Punic Wars from Barnes and Noble that had a simultaneous translation below the original Latin. So I would take my homework assignment, go to the proper paragraph, and copy the translation. After a while, I stopped checking all the words. I verified the first and last sentence of the paragraph, and copied the translation, sometimes adding words in the original that were not in my school text. Father Jablonski caught it once, and approached me in an awed-shocked manner. "Mr. Sciancalepore, I am truly impressed with your knowledge of Latin. You have not only translated the homework assignment, but added some words of your own to give the paragraph a fuller meaning". Everybody laughed, and he never accused me of cheating, but it was clear he never expected much from me, and that I would most likely fail for the year. Boy, did I show him! On the day of the final exam, we were seated in checkerboard fashion, to minimize cheating. I arranged to have the three smartest kids in the class around me. Two in front on my right and left, and one to my rear on the right. It was a long test, and Father Jablonski would occasionally go outside to stretch his legs. During these moments I would check the answers of my forward classmates, who would leave them on their respective left and right, and modify my answers. If their answers didn't agree with each other, I would skip it. When I was finished, I dropped my work sheet, as did my partner to the rear, and we exchanged them. I then compared his answers with those that the guys in front disagreed with, and recorded the best two-out-three. I got the highest grade in the class, and Father Jablonski was really impressed at how much work I had put in to prepare for the final exam, and he told me so in very glowing words. He ALMOST made me feel guilty.

Also in my sophomore year, I learned how to play the clarinet, taking after-school classes. Well, I learned how to play the notes, but playing a tune was another matter. I had no sense of timing. Nevertheless, at the end of the year, I was given the choice of repeating the after-school class, or joining the school marching band in my junior year. It was a regular class, we got uniforms and a school letter, and we played at all the football games. It was no choice at all, and I figured I'd learn to play better by the following year.

Meanwhile, back in the neighborhood, things were moving along nicely. I liked my new friends, and looked forward to hanging out "down the block". We would play boxball, punchball, kick-the-can, Johnny-on-the-pony, three steps to Germany, stoopball, strikeout, and when we had more time, handball, stickball, baseball, football, and basketball.

1947—Richie and the guys

1947—Roddy

I kept in touch with the old neighborhood, and once brought a team with me to challenge them at stickball. We played for money (25-50 cents each), in the high school schoolyard where I used to hang out, and we almost won. Because we didn't have enough guys, Irving played on our team. We were winning until the last inning. With two outs, Irving dropped a deep fly ball, allowing the winning run to score for the other team. All the way home, the guys were on my back about how Irving had "thrown" the game to his buddies. I knew it wasn't true, but I still felt bad because I liked both my old friends and my new ones, and I wanted all of them to do well.

My old buddies did do something that made me proud. Baseball was not their game, but they got a team together, and came up to 243rd to challenge us. We walked up to PS11 in Yonkers together, and played a pretty good game. This was our game, and we did win, but only by one or two runs. To see my old buddies hit, and run around the bases on a field that had grass and wasn't full of pebbles, made me very proud of them. I can still see Carlo trying to score from second base after a hit, charging like a bull elephant, rounding third base, and sliding under the tag at home plate. Where had they learned to play like that? We all walked back together after the game, we were all buddies, and we waived goodbye as they left on the trolley to go back home. I don't remember seeing them again after that. As I said, the houses were torn down for the "projects", my old buddies were scattered, and I never saw any of them again.

If you've noticed that my life was just school and play, and that I'm not as obsessed with girls as before, you're just partly right! We always talked about girls, but opportunities were few, and by sixteen years old, I still hadn't kissed a girl. There was a girl (Ginevra) "down the block" that liked me, but I liked her friend, who couldn't like me because her friend liked me. Anyway, Ginevra hung out with us guys, and even volunteered to be the "pillow" when we played johnny-on-the-pony. The "pillow" was the person that would stand, back to the wall, and act as a cushion to the rest of the team, which would bend over and lock unto the partner's legs in front of them. The opposing team then would run and jump unto this "pony", trying to break the lock. If they couldn't break the lock, or if they fell off, then they would become the "pony".

Genevra at bat

My first kiss

I always saw Genevra as "one of the guys", until she announced she was going to have a sweet-sixteen birthday party, and invited the gang. This was my first "adult" party, and I got all dressed up, and even brought a gift! Actually, my mother bought the gift and dressed me up! I was very nervous. It must have been a first for the other guys and girls too, because we didn't know what to do. The guys got all together on one side of the room, and the girls on the other, divided by a coffee table. Ginevra's mom brought us together by putting hot dogs, with mustard and sauerkraut, on the coffee table. By the time we had the cake, we were pretty friendly, and somebody suggested playing kissing games. I had heard about playing "spin-the-bottle", but they decided to play "this-or-that" (although we pronounced it "dis-or-dat"). Apparently, some of the kids had been to parties before. Anyway, a guy or a girl steps into a closet. The master of ceremonies chooses two kids of the opposite sex, naming one "dis", and the other "dat", then asks the person in the closet if he/she wants "dis" or "dat". The chosen one would then go in the closet, and the couple would kiss. After which, the one who had been in the closet first would leave, and the process would start all over. You can imagine that when the girl you wanted was in the closet, you would signal to the master-of-ceremonies that you wanted to be "dis" or "dat", and to make a special effort to tell the person in the closet to choose you. The girls weren't as outspoken as the guys, but they had their eyes on some of them too. There was a lot of dealing going on, since the person who came out of the closet became the master of ceremonies (you get me in with so-and-so, and I'll get you in with so-and-so). That's how I got my first kiss from Genevra's friend. She was in the closet, and was offered "dis . . . . or THAAAAAAAAT". Nervous as hell, I stepped into the closet, closed the door, and we kissed! What a disappointment! I tasted greasy lipstick, and smelled the hot dogs and sauerkraut on her breath. Then she was gone. I have to admit though, that after a few rounds, the lipstick had worn off, and so had the hot dog smell, and the kissing was good. Genevra got me, and we also got to play spin-the-bottle. It was a fun night, and I felt like I had just passed a major hurdle in my life.

All this school and play was fine with me, but it was causing problems at home. My father, who had been working for as long as he could remember, couldn't conceive of getting tired and dirty and sweated with no money to show for it. Even worse, I would go out to play after school, and would invariably come home late for dinner, which was inexcusable. It became almost a ritual. I would come home, and stand in the doorway to the kitchen. Seated at the table with my mother and brother, having already started eating, my father would yell at me, and then call on the Saints (one by one) to help him with me. When they didn't materialize, he took matters in his own hands. Whatever was close at hand that wouldn't break, he would throw at me. Bread, silverware, breadbasket, cheesegrater, would come at me while I stood in the doorway. After picking all the items up from the floor, and returning them to the table, I could sit and start eating my own meal. Sometimes, before the end of the meal, he would work himself up again at my ingratitude. On these instances, his weapon of choice was the tin cheesegrater. He would raise it and try to hit me in the head with it, but would get my right elbow, which I had raised in self-defense. He would then spend time after dinner, tapping flat the lump on the bottom of the container with a small hammer. When things had calmed down, we were able to look back on those days and joke about it. Even my father saw the humor in it. He never physically hit me again, after the air raid episode, even though God knows I really deserved it many times.

The funniest was one time that I was so late, I missed dinner altogether. As was the custom, we would go downstairs after dinner, or they would come upstairs. This time, I came home to find the table cleared, with uncle Larry, aunt Clara, my mother, father, and brother seated around it. I knew I was in trouble, but was surprised that they barely acknowledged my arrival. I knew there was something going on, but I had no choice, so I started to cautiously make my way into the kitchen. My father chose this time to notice that the kitchen floor needed sweeping around where he was sitting, so he got up and started sweeping near his chair, all the time continuing his conversation with his brother. It didn't look good, but he was totally ignoring me! I had no choice! I had to go ahead! I had just passed behind aunt Clara, with the idea to take a look in the refrigerator. Now I was in range, and out of the corner my eye I saw my father raise the broom, with the idea to smash me with it. I quickly backed up to get out of the kitchen. My father realized that I might get away from his wrath, so instead of following me around the back of aunt Clara's chair, he swung the broom at me. He missed me, lost his footing, and wound up draped across aunt Clara's lap, still holding the broom. It was very funny recalling it later, but not at the time. I had to wait outside on the porch until after he went to bed. Then my mother called me up, and fed me dinner

My Junior and Senior years at Cardinal Hayes were memorable not for my studies, but for my continued run-ins with Father Jablonski, who had now become Dean of Discipline. I also got involved with school teams, joining the track team and the handball team. I never tried out for the baseball, football, or basketball teams, because I didn't think I was good enough, but I more than held my own in the intra-murals in school. Part of the reason was that it was a 45-minute commute by train from home, which wouldn't leave much time to hang out in the neighborhood, but mostly it was that these were new sports for me, and I needed more time. A few days a week I would take a very early train, and get to school about 7 AM. Then I would go to the gym, change, and practice basketball in the semi-dark, fantasizing that the coach would also come in early, be impressed with my dedication, and put me on the team. It never happened, but I did improve, and I was a top player on our neighborhood team.

First things first. I started my junior year as a member of the school band, considered to be one of the best in the city. This was because Fr. Zemak was gifted, but also a strict disciplinarian. He wasn't as careful with his personal appearance as he was with his band, and he was a very intimidating person. Overweight, a heavy smoker, maybe an alcoholic, he could curse with the best of them, or so it was said.

It was an honor to be on the band. It was a regular class, we had uniforms, and we played at school functions, parades in the city, and at all the football games. Unfortunately, I was not musically inclined. I could play the notes, but I had no rhythm, and was lost after the first bar. I would then try to guess as to where the rest of the band was, and would skip ahead, with no clue. In my defense, as 3rd clarinet, I did not play the melody, and had some justification for getting lost. The fact was that I contributed absolutely nothing to the band. Fortunately, in a 110-piece band, it was easy to hide. Plus, I took advantage of opportunities, like playing the tuba. No, I had no idea how to play that instrument either, but the band had four tubas, and needed a fifth. This because each tuba opening (I'm sure there's a name for it) had a school letter over it, so that when we marched it advertised we were from H-A-Y-E-S. I volunteered for the duty, which excused me from playing clarinet, and also made some brownie points with Fr. Zemak. Even here though, I got into trouble. Fr. Zemak expressly told me to only make believe I was playing, but not to actually make any sounds. Well, I behaved at the beginning of the football game, during the halftime show on the field, and almost to the end of the game, but temptation got the better of me. It was cold, but the big tuba mouthpiece was keeping my lips warm. Our team was on a drive to score a touchdown, and after a big gain, the band would play a brief rally refrain. I got all excited, and decided to participate. With all the noise, and such a big band, I figured nobody would notice. So, at the next opportunity, when the band started, I gave a hearty blow and pressed a couple of keys. Unfortunately, I was the only tuba that made any sound, and the sound wasn't very pretty. Fr. Zemak looked like he had just been shot, huffed and puffed up the stands to where I was, and gave me a couple of solid shots in the head with the music books he was carrying. Maybe he figured I could learn something if he hit me hard enough with the books.

One way or another, believe it or not, I made it to the end of the year. Well, almost to the end. During the final exams, the seniors were excused from class, and our class was reduced to less than half its size. For the first time, I found myself with no place to hide. There was only one 1st clarinet, one 2nd, and only me as 3rd clarinet. I made believe I was playing, but made no sounds. Fr. Zemak looked in my direction, puzzled as to why he wasn't hearing what he was supposed to hear. He signaled the band to continue playing, laboriously got down from his podium, and wheezed his way to my chair. Now I had no choice. I had no idea where we were musically, so I picked a spot on the sheet, started to play those notes, and prayed to God for a miraculous intervention. God wasn't listening to me that particular day, but Fr. Zemak was, and he couldn't believe what he was hearing. He forced himself to bend over so his ear was directly at the end of my instrument, while I just kept playing as if nothing was wrong. When he straightened up, I could see by his expression that he realized I had put one over on him for a whole year. With a backhanded swing, he sent my chair, and me with clarinet still firmly in my mouth, on a beautiful back flip unto the floor. As I scrambled to my feet, he pointed to the door, and said "out". To help me along, he lifted his cassock, and kicked me in the rear, and he kept kicking me all the way to the door. With every kick, I gave a little jump, so it must have looked like I was doing the bunny hop across the room. The final indignity was that after I had opened the door, his last kick launched me headfirst into the door edge. The class was in an uproar, and I never set foot in there again. I had the last laugh, though. He didn't fail me (as a matter of fact, I think I got a B), and I got my school letter.

Fr. Jablonski was something else. He already knew me from Latin II, and he was ready for me. Actually, he was ready for everybody, and took on the whole student body when he became Dean of Discipline. He seemed to have a sadistic streak in him, and enjoyed torturing us. Actually, I never saw him that way. He was tough, but we deserved whatever we got. I enjoyed my running battles with him, and I won some and lost some. "Jabo" was a favorite of his time and has become school lore.

For example, he was in charge of the "late room", more popularly known as "jug". If you were late for school, misbehaved in class, or needed some kind mild punishment, you would spend and hour after school in "jug". Since I tended to qualify in all of those areas, I almost had a reserved seat in "jug". It wasn't all that bad, because you could do some homework there. Well, you could, if you behaved yourself. Meaning, there was a basic rule of no talking to each other. "Jabo" would explain the rules at the beginning, and advised that if we would do well in the first half hour, we could study for the last half hour. Then he would wander outside the class, and leave us all alone. Invariably, some idiot couldn't refrain from whispering something to his buddy, not knowing that Fr. Jablonski had come back in from the other door, and was standing in the back of the class. He would then come to the front, and with hands over his heart, would say, "See, it's not me. You knew what you had to do, and you didn't do it. Now you can all stand up instead of sitting for the next fifteen minutes". Variations of these tests made "jug" not a place to want to go to, and it wasn't unusual for the hour to be extended for another ½—1 hour, if the natives were restless.

He seemed to derive particular pleasure in the morning, standing outside the front door to the school, watching the arriving students run so as to get in before the starting bell. When it got close, he would yell to those that were further back not to run any more, because they weren't going to make it. Of course, instead of taking his advice, they would try to speed up, but were hampered by the heavy school bags they had to carry. Then he would loudly start the countdown, "Ten seconds . . . nine . . . eight . . . ." It was a sight to see, especially when he would shut the door exactly at "zero", put on the most angelic smile you'd ever want to see, and say to the panting students, "See, I told you that you weren't going to make it. You should have listened. I'm really your friend."

I was almost never a party to that frenzy. Early on, I realized I had to have an alternate plan. Leaving home earlier was one, but I didn't do it consistently enough. So, I made sure that one of the windows in the gym locker room was unlocked, and when I was just a little late, I would go around the back of the school, down the back stairs, open the unlocked window, and make it upstairs before the first attendance was taken. I saved myself many "jug" days.

When my brother followed me to Cardinal Hayes, (I graduated in '49, and he in '56), I shared my secret with him. However, he didn't follow the instructions fully. When he was late, instead of going around the back of the school, he still tried to run and make it through the front door. When he realized he wasn't going to make it, he crossed the Grand Concourse in front of the school, then crossed back when he got to the far side, and then made his way to the back stairs leading to the gym locker room. "Jabo" was still doing his thing at the front door, and followed Mike's movement. So it happened that after Mike had opened the window, and had one leg in and one leg out, he heard "Jabo" say, "So, Sciancalepore, you don't like to come in the front door like all the other students? No, no, don't come back out! If that's the way you want to come into school, go right ahead. You go right on in, and right upstairs, and I'll see you in my office." It was one of the few times Mike was ever in trouble. He was as good as I was bad. He also joined the band, but played on the swing band, which were the best players in the school, playing both clarinet and saxophone. He used that experience to start his own band, and they were very good.

One day in his junior year, he was sick at home, and Fr. Jablonski called to make sure he wasn't a truant. It just so happened that I was home for lunch from work, and answered the phone. When he realized it was me, he started grilling me as to why I wasn't working. Six years after graduation, and he got me all tongue-tied, especially when he said, "Are you sure your brother's sick in bed? Do I have to speak to him"? "No Father, he's really here . . . he's really sick. No, I'm really working. I'm just home for lunch". Thankfully, he let me go. Great guy. Became Monsignor, and in later years, always came back to visit with the alumni during special event days.

When he was particularly upset, he would send you home and say, "Come back with your mother". My mother and he got to know each other pretty well, and the conversation would go something like: "Vito has not been a good boy"—"I know, Father"—"What are going to do with him"?—"I don't know, Father"—"Don't worry Mrs. Sciancalepore, I'll take care of it"—"Thank-you Father". Then to me, "I'll see you in jug".

There was one time I put one over him, and he knew it. I had a big test that I wasn't prepared for, and I wanted to get out of it. So, I broke one of the lenses from my eyeglasses, and went to his office. I explained that I had a big test, but I couldn't see the blackboard without my eyeglasses. Fortunately, my Optometrist was only a few blocks away on 149th Street, and I could have my lens replaced and be back in time for the test. He grumbled, but gave me permission to go, so long as I would be back in two hours. I went, and my glasses were ready in an hour. I waited another hour before calling Jabo, and telling him that the Optometrist didn't have my lens and had sent out for them. We expected delivery any minute, and I should be back at school within the hour. However, if he wanted me to, I would come back now, since he had only given me two hours. He asked me if I was sure it would only take another hour, and then gave me the OK. Thank God, otherwise I would have had to break my lens again. I waited about and hour fifteen minutes before calling back. I apologized for the delay, but my glasses had just gotten done, and I was on my way back to school. I then pointed out to him that I wouldn't be back for another twenty minutes. I had already missed the test, and school was over in an hour. I asked if maybe he wouldn't excuse for the rest of the day, and I promised I would make up for any lost work. He asked to speak to the Optometrist, but I told him I had left the store five minutes ago, and was calling from a public phone. If he wanted me to, I would go back to the store, and have the Optometrist call him. There was a long silence, followed by a longer sigh, and then, "Alright Sciancalepore, you did it to me this time, but I'm gonna remember you for this. Go home". I protested about how I disappointed I was, not being able to make it back on time, especially since I had studied so hard for the test, and I was really ready for it. All he said was, "Yeah yeah yeah, I'll see you tomorrow". I knew that he knew that I had pulled a fast one on him, and he was not going to forget it, but I had gotten out of taking a test I wasn't ready for, and tomorrow is another day.

I did do some constructive things while at Cardinal Hayes. My grades were good. I was a solid B student. I also joined the track team and the handball team. Handball didn't last too long, but track was year-round. I especially liked running cross-country at Van Courtland Park, about 2 ½ or 3 ½ miles. After the start, about 300 guys would dash across an open plain, trying to get the best position before reaching the woods, and a lot of ups and downs on ground covered with dead leaves, where it was easy to twist an ankle. I was always ready to quit after the opening dash, not knowing how I was ever going to make it to the end. Somehow, I never stopped, and somewhere around mid-course I got my second wind. A lot of guys on a narrow trail, and no matter how many I passed, there were still a lot more in front. We would come out of the woods for the last half-mile to the finish line, and I always had a big finishing kick, of which I was very proud. My coach didn't see it that way. He felt I should have used some of that energy earlier, finishing more tired but closer to the leaders. He was probably right, but I felt I had given it all I had. I always finished in the teens, and my best was 7th, which was not good enough for a medal. In a field of 300+, I thought it was very good.

In the indoor season, I ran the mile and the mile relay, and I didn't win any medals there either. In the mile, I did as the coach suggested, and gave everything I had from the beginning. By the last quarter mile, I was pumping as hard as I could, but I was not going as fast, and would finish in the middle of the pack. One time, racing at Madison Square Garden, I thought I had a chance. It was a big meet, and the student body turned out in force. I was entered in the mile, which was like 16 times around a raised and banked wooden track. The track put an extra spring in my legs, and the cheers from the stands gave me extra strength. Unfortunately, they were all sitting in the same section of stands. I found myself racing as fast as I could when I passed that section, pushed along by their yells, only to fall back again at the other end of the track. Didn't win any medals in the indoor season either, but I enjoyed the experience.

Back in the neighborhood, we had a team for every season. Baseball, football, and basketball, named The Devils. Not much equipment, but we didn't need much, except for football. That's why we only competed in football for one year. Plus, we were nice guys, but the teams we played were really tough guys, or at least tougher than us.

For example, we played a bunch of guys called "Fadigadi's Team", and their star player was, of course, Fadigadi. They all had equipment, and they all cursed a lot, but Fadigadi was bigger and cursed using some very bad words. When they had the ball, he would come charging through the line, cursing at all of us, and telling what he would do to the guy who would dare tackle him. I was very proud of our team. We went after him anyway, getting straight-armed, butted by his helmet, bouncing off his padded pants, and trying to not get run over by his cleated shoes. We had none of that equipment, and got beaten badly. I don't think we scored a point.

Another time, all the other guys on the front line had helmets. We had maybe five guys altogether with a helmet, and I wasn't one of them. Elmer was another one, and he was on the line. Amazingly, Elmer took on the guy across from him, and more than held his own. Every time the ball was snapped, Elmer would go after the opposing lineman, and it looked like two bulls colliding. After the game, Elmer felt dizzy, and while biking home from Yonkers, we stopped almost at every drugstore, so Elmer could buy an aspirin for his headache. We called him Elmer Fudd, because he really wasn't too "swift". Fortunately, he recovered. That was also the game I was tackled, after a long run, and twisted my left knee. I also recovered.

Our last game was the one in which I had my nose broken. Playing halfback, I carried the ball through the line, where I was tackled by a couple of guys. As I was falling forward to the ground, my arms were pinned to my sides, unable to soften the landing, and unable to get out of the way of an upcoming knee from a fallen player. It got me right in the nose. I felt a crack, and it started bleeding immediately. We called a time-out to stuff my nose, and then restarted the game. Since we didn't have any extra players, I stayed in the game. You would imagine I would have gotten some consideration for my injury, but you would be wrong. Instead, every time I would carry the ball, they would come after me, all the while yelling, "Hit him in the nose . . . hit him in the nose!!!" Very unnerving, especially since my nose started bleeding again, and was staining my clothes. I got out and we finished the game with ten players. We never played another game, and I've carried that broken nose with me to this day. There was never a question of getting it fixed. It was only a broken nose, and it didn't look too bad.

Baseball was something else. We were actually pretty good, and after a couple of years, we decided to get uniforms. We went to the printer, and ordered a few hundred raffle books. We sold the tickets for ten cents each, and had a grand prize of $25 dollars. We sold about $150, and when the day came for the drawing, we had a big ceremony at the clubhouse, and drew the winner. We really didn't have to do it, because other than the date of the drawing, there was no information on the raffle ticket. However, we realized it was the honorable thing to do. Besides, we figured one of us would win. Disappointingly, the winner was someone we didn't know. So, Richie, Roddy, and myself, took the $25 prize to the address of the winner. At least, we figured we'd make somebody happy that day. However, that fortunate lady wasn't home at the time of our visit, and no one answered the doorbell. After a few tries, we consulted on what to do. The decision was unanimous! The good lady had missed her opportunity, and we were going to keep the money! She would never know what she had missed, and certainly could not be unhappy about it. We, on the other hand, would have an extra $25 for balls and equipment. We had wanted to make someone happy that day, and we did. We were delirious! However, having made the decision, we were not totally out of the woods. The lady lived in an apartment, and she could come back at any time. We had to get out as quickly as possible, and not speak to anyone on the way, because it might be the missing lady. You can't imagine the anxiety on the way out of that building, or the joy when we got back to the clubhouse, and shared the good news. We renamed the team, from the Devils to Pontiacs, after an Indian tribe, and got uniforms with blue lettering.

Mickey Carjulo, Johny Salzman, Ed Blough, Walt Gargar, Roddy, Carjulo
Ernie Muller, me, Richie, Jerry Gilberg, Stevey Zimmerman, Carjulo Jr.

Our team was made up of players from our block, but also from Yonkers, and other neighborhoods. However, we were the core, and I was elected captain. We played all over the Bronx, Yonkers, and Mount Vernon. We were pretty good, winning many more than we lost. Richie was our main pitcher, Roddy was a very good shortstop, and I was the center fielder. Joe DiMaggio was my hero, and Ted Williams was a close second, although defensively I liked Joe's brother on the Red Sox, Dom DiMaggio. Occasionally, Richie, Roddy, and I, would go see games at Yankee Stadium, especially when the Red Sox were in town. That was the team of DiMaggio, King Kong Keller, Tommy Henrich, Phil Rizzuto, and Yogi Berra (although he started his career as Larry, and played right field). I also used to go to games by myself, sit in the bleachers, and study how the guys played in the outfield. It was very cheap, and a great way to pass an afternoon (there were no night games).

I mentioned a clubhouse before. Yes, we had clubhouse, and it was neat! It was right on the main street of White Plains Road, across from 243rd Street, where we lived. Originally, it had been the office for a used-car lot, which had gone out of business. It was a wooden shed on pilings, about three feet off the ground. Inside, it was about 8x10 feet, with a small covered porch outside.

We asked the real estate office that had the lot for sale if we could use it for a clubhouse. He checked with the owner, and amazingly got an OK. We redecorated the inside with girlie pictures, and built personal bunks for Richie, Roddy, and myself. Richie, who would go on to become an engineer, designed a secret way to lock/unlock the door. Using pulleys and a rope, a 2x4 would bolt/unbolt the door from the inside. The ends of the rope were hidden behind one of the outside shingles. We also built and emergency escape-hatch in the floor, in case we were ever attacked (I don't know from what). In spite of the secret lock, one day we found the door unlocked, and a bum sleeping inside (today you would call him a homeless person). Although it was our personal place, we shared it with the guys on the block, and it was our "hangout". It had no heat or electricity, and it was very cold in the winter, but we made do with a kerosene lantern.

It lasted maybe a year-and-a-half. One night, my parents and Mike came home (I think from the movies), and told me that firemen were all over the clubhouse. I ran down the block, to indeed see a fireman on the roof, punching a hole with his ax, while others were axing the walls and hosing it down, surrounded by stinky black smoke. I saw no flames, but when they were finished, so was our clubhouse. I never found out who was responsible, but it must have been somebody who broke in. Richie and Roddy certainly knew better.

Mike also took the loss very personal. After all, he was the team mascot and batboy, and he took his duties very seriously. Now about ten years old, he came to most of our games, and took care of the equipment. The bag holding the bats was almost as big as he was, and it was a sight to see him struggle with it, going and coming from games, but those bats were always in order on the side of the field. He hung out with us at the clubhouse, played some of the games we played, and sometimes was the object of the game. Like the time we rolled him up with a mattress, and threw him off the porch. He wasn't hurt at all. Even then, he was having "Mikey" stories, like the time we were playing hide-and-seek. Mike found a great hiding spot, under the clubhouse, behind a bush. Figured nobody would find him, and nobody did. However, the guy who was "it", decided to take a pee-break, and where did he decide to do pee-pee? Yes . . . right into the bush that Mike was hiding behind! Did Mike run out? No-sireee! He toughed it out, because he didn't want to get caught and be "it".

While I'm on the subject of Mike, I may as well confess to something that I thought was funny at the time, but of which I've been ashamed since.

For some occasion, Mike got a piggy bank, except it was a baby-doll bank about a foot tall. The only opening was in the top of the head, and the grownups missed no opportunity to stuff money in there. The only way to get the money out would be to break the figurine, and they would do that in a few years, after it had been filled up. Now, as a late teenager, I was always short on money. True, I was getting a six-dollar-a-week allowance (nobody I knew was getting any more than two), and I also had income from part-time jobs, but I always spent more than I had. That doll, pregnant with all that loot, kept smiling at me from the top of the dresser closet. Actually, I figured it was really laughing at me.

So it came to pass that the temptation became a challenge. Besides, it wasn't like I was stealing the money. I was just borrowing it, and I would certainly return it before they opened the doll in a few years.

I found that if I turned the doll upside down, and slid a knife up and down inside the opening, I could get bills and coins to slide out. So, whenever I was short of cash, I would "borrow" some money from the doll, which wasn't laughing at me any more. At first, I only took the bills (about five dollars at a time). Then the silver. I returned any pennies that came out. Woe is me! Time passed, and unexpectedly, they decided to open the doll. My father broke the doll with a hammer, and the coins lay all about. There wasn't a single dollar bill, and I also don't remember any silver coins. The look of astonishment on my father's face was something to behold. While on one level I knew I was in trouble, on another level I had a sense of accomplishment. I had gotten all the good stuff. I hadn't missed anything! However, the look that bothered me most then, and to this day, was the one on Mike's face. The happy anticipation was replaced by surprise and disappointment. He counted all the pennies, and I'm sure he could tell you today what the total was. I confessed, and thought it was very funny. Again, I don't recall being punished, but after a few years I stopped seeing the humor, and haven't liked myself for that behavior. No, I never repaid Mike the money.

Mike was a very good boy; as good as I was bad. He was well behaved, studious, and cute. He kept my mother company when she went shopping, and would run errands for her after being asked just once. I liked taking him with me to the Saturday morning movies. They played ten cartoons, and a full-length movie for kids. By the time we got out, it was late afternoon, and time for dinner. We would walk home from the RKO movie house in Mount

Vernon. I always remembered how much I enjoyed when zio Amerigo took me when he went out with his friends to the movies or a restaurant, and I hoped Mike would feel the same way. After all, the eight-year age difference made me a very old older brother!

Of course, that wouldn't stop me from having fun with him, and here's another "Mikey" story: We shared a bedroom, and he was 8-9 years old. I don't know why, except maybe since we had played that Superman game when we lived on Cortland Ave, I told him I had a secret that I would share with him, if he promised not to tell anyone. The sincere look on his face was something to behold, as he promised that he would not tell a soul. So was the look of surprise when I told him I was really Superman. I told him I was out every night, flying around the city, doing all sorts of good deeds. He balked at this, pointing out that I was in the bed next to his, and he saw me there. I told him it was not really me, but an image of me that I left behind, so nobody would suspect. He trusted me, and bought the story so totally, that he never even asked me to show him some little proof of my powers.

True to his word, he kept the secret . . . for a full two weeks! Then, puffed with pride as to the true identity of his brother, he found he had to share the secret with someone. Unfortunately, the kid he chose for the momentous disclosure was the biggest smart-ass in the neighborhood. After Mike had gotten him to swear eternal silence, he told him the big news. When the kid started to laugh, Mike was insulted and figured that maybe he shouldn't have confided in him. When the kid still couldn't stop laughing ten minutes later, Mike started to have second thoughts about his own commitment. I don't know who he went to next, maybe our mother, but my cover was blown. Aside from being very funny, to me it's always been an example of the high regard he held me in. He was a great kid.

*　　*　　*

The car accident—

The event that was very bad, but could have been disastrous, was the car accident. Car malfunction would be a better description. I was the only one not involved, because I had a date, and didn't go. My brother reminded me of the finer details.

It was late '47 or early '48. Uncle Larry had bought a used limousine that didn't work, and brought it in to Chrysler to have it fixed up. It was the first family car, if you don't count uncle Larry's ice truck, and it was decided to celebrate by taking a trip to Brooklyn to visit the Gatto's, who were family friends, and my godparents. The car was very large, with plenty of room. Uncle Larry and aunt Clara up front, Mike and Christine in the pull-up seats behind the limo partition, and my mother and father in the back.

They left about 11 AM on a Sunday morning, but ran into trouble on the Belt Parkway. The rear wheel began to smoke, and uncle Larry pulled over to take a look a couple of times. Deciding it was something he had to get fixed on Monday, he continued on, not realizing he was losing his brakes. So it happened that when he saw traffic stopped up ahead, he pushed on the brakes, and nothing happened. He didn't want to go smashing into those cars, so he swerved to the right, off the road, and down an embankment. That particular section had some wooden barricades, because they were building an overpass. Uncle Larry figured to slow down on the open ground on the way to the overpass wall. Actually, he didn't lose much speed, and he hadn't noticed the big hole in front of the wall. It takes longer to tell than the seconds he actually had to decide. The car went nose-first into that hole, which was about 6-8 feet deep, and everybody was injured, except Mike. At the last minute, he saw uncle Larry with one hand on the steering wheel, and the other arm up, so he did the same thing, and put his head on his arm on the partition in front of him. Other than a bruised and swollen arm, he was fine. Not so the others. Uncle Larry had broken the steering wheel on impact, and was lucky that the metal horn ring protruding from it had not punctured his throat, but just scratched it. Aunt Clara had internal injuries, and had to be pulled out by people who came to help. Chris was passed out, pinned under her folding seat, and wound up with a broken collarbone. My father broke his glasses on the back of Mike's seat, and was bleeding from his forehead. My mother went over Chris, and smashed her face on the hard partition behind the front seat. It almost severed her nose off her face. It was hanging on by about an inch at the bottom.

They had to be helped out of the car, and lifted out of the hole. My mother, with handkerchiefs holding her nose to her face, was bleeding profusely, and was gulping down the blood, thinking it would help stop the loss (it wouldn't have). She was very weak, but didn't pass out. Holding nose to face, she went around to see how the others were doing. Mike remembers uncle Larry "going nuts". It was maybe the only time in his life that he was not in control of himself.

The ambulances took everyone but uncle Larry and Mike to the hospital, and someone gave them a ride there. Uncle Larry called our family doctor, Dr Anthony Cerrato, from the hospital, and he drove out right away. He raised hell to get them proper care, arranged to have them moved to our local hospital the next day, and then drove Mike, my father, and uncle Larry home. The next day he was back, and drove us to the hospital.

I don't know if I'll get to spend some time talking about Dr. Cerrato, so let me mention now what a truly special person and doctor he was. He made house calls, even when all other doctors stopped. Many years later, when my father was in his 80's, I asked him why, considering he was also getting on in years. He said, "Do you think your father would understand, if after all these years, I would tell him that he would have to come to see me, instead of the other way around? He would get very upset. No, my patients are my sheep, and we're all going to get older together." He was the kind of family doctor you would see on TV. You could call him anytime, and he was always there.

When Marco was an infant, we took him to a Jewish Pediatrician, who had no experience with babies that were not circumcised, who "cleaned" his penis. Later that evening, we saw the penis had swollen to several times its size. The doctor was not available. Panic-stricken, we called Dr. Cerrato's service, and he immediately called back. We explained the situation, and he said he would be right over. He showed up shortly, dressed in a tuxedo. He had been at a formal family dinner party when contacted. He pulled the skin back over the swollen part, and said everything would be fine by morning. He even tried to make us feel better by saying he would only miss dessert, and they would save him a piece. He was a great help to an immigrant family that entrusted him with their care. Hopefully, I'll get to mention him again.

My mother required surgery to put her nose back in place, but her face had been transformed, and was never the same. Thankfully, there had been no deaths, and that was my basic reaction. I was shocked to see my father and uncle in bandages when I got home, but so long as no one had gotten killed, I figured everything else would work out. However, my mother's face was a constant reminder of that day.

*   *   *

Around 1947 my world finally expanded to include girls. Well, I mean live girls! We always talked about them, and Richie, Roddy, and I would fantasize about what kind of girl we would meet, and what our lives would be like if and when that would happen. Otherwise, it was baseball, basketball, games down the block, and the movies.

It was after seeing a movie, that a bunch of us were walking home, and passed a house with some girls looking out of an open window from a raised 1st floor apartment. They were having a slumber party, and we started to talk to them. Amazingly, they answered back! That had never happened before! Even more amazing, the parents came to the window, and invited us in! There must have been about eight girls, and I remember Noreen and her sister Maureen, Ginger, a couple of others, and Jeannie.

I always associate that experience with Walt Disney's "Bambi". You remember when Bambi, Thumper, and Flower were walking in the fields in the spring? Thumper was attracted by a girl bunny, and disappeared. Flower likewise. Puzzled, Bambi asked Mr. Owl what was going on? Mr. Owl explained that they had been "peeter-paited" (or some such word—I'll correct it if I get the chance). Well, since I see myself as Bambi, this was the occasion when my Thumper (Richie) was "peeter-paited" by Jeannie. No-doubt-about-it-love-at-first-sight kind of thing. They just had eyes for each other, but unlike in "Bambi", they did not disappear. They became the anchor that brought the rest of the guys and girls together, and we would regularly walk to 238th Street to hang out with them.

Other than Richie and Jeannie, there was no other coupling off. I liked Ginger, but she liked one of the other guys. Eventually, I did get a girl of my own, and I would go visit when she was babysitting for money. Some kissing, but nothing serious, and I don't remember her name. However, we now had a group that included girls, and it was more fun. They came to watch us play basketball, and we did things together. Richie's mother had bought him a car (I think it was a '38 Ford). I also had a '35 jalopy with a rumble seat. One day we decided to go on a picnic upstate to Poughkeepsie, and piled everybody into the two cars and went. Bad decision! My car engine started to smoke, and began losing oil. Instead of turning back, we stuck chewing gum on the engine crack, and bought ten quarts of used oil from the gas station. Occasionally, we would stop and pour some oil into the engine. Elmer was in charge of chewing gum to replace the wad that kept falling off. In this way we made it up to Poughkeepsie, found a grassy field with a running stream, played, and had a nice picnic.

On the way home, we continued the same routine with my car, but we started losing more oil than we were putting in, and then it gave up. After a big "BOOM", a black mushroom cloud rose from the hood of the car, and it came to a stop. We pushed it to the side of the highway, and saw a big hole in the side of the engine. We were stuck far away from home, and a couple of the girls started to cry. The parents didn't know where they were, and they would be in big trouble if they didn't get back in time. We left the girls by the car and were lucky to find a junkyard down the road. Richie then piled the girls in his car and drove them home, after which he would come back and pick us up from the junkyard. We pushed the car to the yard and got $15 for it. Then we waited for Richie. It was dark when he came back, but everything worked out OK, except for the loss of the car.

That wasn't my first car. The year before, aunt Clara's brother Phil had stopped by the house with an old car he had borrowed from somebody in Harlem, who wanted to sell it for $50. What a deal, I thought. Of course, I convinced my mother. She had $30, we borrowed $20 from aunt Clara, and we had our first car. Insurance wasn't mandatory, so there was no other expense. The guy had left the plates on the car. I also didn't have a license, and wasn't old enough to drive anyway. Details that I would take care of later, I assured everyone.

When my father came home from work, and we shared our good news, we didn't get the reception we expected. Maybe we should have waited until he had come into the apartment and settled down, instead of springing it on him as he entered the door. Apparently, this was just too much for him. Dropping his tools, and looking straight at me, he said, "You're trying to drive me crazy", over and over again. For punctuation, after each time, he would hit the side of his head against the wall on which he was leaning. He worked himself up so much, that he skipped dinner and went straight to bed. However, the banging he had given himself had given him a major headache, and he couldn't sleep. He kept calling for my mother to bring him another aspirin, and we could hear the mumbling from the kitchen.

When I got up the next morning, I found my father already in the kitchen. My mother said he had gotten up very early to take a look at the car, and had made the observation that with a little fixing up, it was a nice car. Go figure!

Didn't get much use out of that car. Two of the doors didn't work, and it needed a paint job. I decided to paint it myself, and sanded it down to the metal first. Not the whole car, but the trunk first. That was enough to convince me it was a lot of work and more than I could handle, so I stopped.

Of course, the exposed metal began to rust, and the car looked even worse. So, with the exception of a sneaked ride now and then, the car sat in front of the house, where Richie, Roddy, and I would sit and ponder life.

*   *   *

Vilma Coletti-my first grown-up-serious-girlfriend:

Standing in the rear of a movie theatre, we struck up a conversation with a couple of girls, and after the movie, Richie, Roddy, and I walked them home. I couldn't get one of the girls out of my mind, and a few weeks later I got up enough courage to go to her house on 229th Street. It was a three-story building and I didn't know her last name, so I rang all the bells, and stood at the bottom of the stairs asking to speak to Vilma. Eventually she showed up, and had no idea who I was. Obviously, I hadn't made as big an impression on her, but soon remembered, and invited me upstairs. I met the mother, and was further captivated. Vilma was a first-generation American like me, the parents were from Venice, and still spoke Italian to the daughter. The musical tone of the Venetian dialect was intoxicating. In fact, everything about the girl was so positive, I would have proposed marriage on the spot. Of course that couldn't be, but I was sure I had found my life-partner. The fact that I didn't know anything about her didn't matter. I had that feeling. Of course I had had that feeling with Lucy, Mary Rapetti, and others, but this was the real thing!

We went out a couple of times, to a movie or for an ice cream, and it was great, until she told me about what she wanted to do with her life. She wanted to work, and she wanted to become a nurse! My God, this was not acceptable! I figured I should be the center of her universe, with no need for her to work. I would provide, although I didn't have a clue about how. The worst part though, was her being a <u>nurse</u>! To me, that meant that she would see and tend to naked men other than myself! Totally out of the question! I tried to talk her out of it, but she was committed. So, our relationship cooled, but I've always thought I made more out of it than she did. I wrote to her when I was in Italy, and even double-dated with Mario when I came back, but it was not to be.

She did become a nurse, and shortly before I was to be married, I ran into her. She and another nurse were waiting for a bus after work at a hospital in Mt. Vernon, when I passed in my car. I gave them a ride home, and Vilma told her friend what a great catch I would be for some girl. I can't deny I derived a little bit of pleasure from informing them that I had already been snagged, and that I had a business in Italy, where we would be going to after getting married. I've always felt a little bad about the way I said that, but she's the one who brought up the subject. Besides, I still think I cared more for her than she did for me.

Vilma will always have a special place in my heart. She was my first serious girlfriend. By a strange coincidence that I found out about many many years later, her cousin Mary married my cousin Vito. I was told that she had married, her husband owned a restaurant, and had children. Unfortunately, her husband had died, and she was living somewhere in Yonkers.

* * *

My jobs:

I don't want to give the impression that my teenage years were all play and getting into trouble, although it wouldn't be far from wrong. I did have part-time work, and it's worth mentioning if only because of the ease with which I found work, and the high regard my employers had of me. Well, at least at the beginning.

My first job was delivering groceries for a Jewish grocery store before we moved to 243rd Street, which I've already mentioned. Next was delivering newspapers. There was no home newspaper delivery in our area, so Richie, Roddy, and I took a trolley (no, did not hitch-hike on the back) about 20 minutes away to Fordham Road, where there were a lot buildings. We picked up "The Bronx Home News", and delivered it to assigned apartments in the area. Once a week we collected, but we had to pay for the newspapers in advance. Some people weren't home when we collected, and not all tipped. Considering the time involved, and deducting the cost of the trolley to go back and forth, we were only earning a couple of dollars a week at best. My allowance was much more than what I earned, and that job didn't last very long.

On the corner of 243rd Street was a pharmacy, and Mr. Friedman was the druggist. He was a very nice man (Jewish, short, and bald), who never bothered us kids that hung out outside. Consider that we played ball against his wall, and climbed on the drugstore roof to retrieve balls that went there, yet he never told us to stop. He and his wife lived in the same building as Richie, across from the store. I think my mother asked him if he had a job for me, and he hired me for a few days a week. I don't remember him having any kids from the neighborhood before me, and I was sort of proud to get it. While the other guys were just hanging out doing nothing, I had a job that required a certain degree of trust, and I felt like a big deal. Plus, it paid double my allowance. In fact, my job was mostly rearranging shelves in the store, as well as the stored merchandise in the basement. I would also wait on customers if Mr. Friedman was filling prescriptions, but my favorite job was helping him fill those prescriptions. He would dole out the necessary ingredients, and then I would mix and grind it into a fine powder in a cup with a pestle. Then I would fill as many gelatin capsules as were necessary. Occasionally, he would send me up to his apartment to run an errand for Mrs. Friedman, who was also a very nice woman. I had the run of the store, it was a position of trust, and I didn't abuse it. Well, there was one exception. When working down in the basement, there was so much extra stuff, and there was always the temptation to take some. The one I couldn't resist was a small glass lantern, filled with a liquid fragrance and a wick that would burn it into the air. I snuck it out with the garbage, but I didn't enjoy it as much as I thought I would. It was a small thing, but it was still a betrayal of trust, and it bothered me. Anyway, I must have left a favorable impression, because later on he also hired Mike for the same work. Maybe that's where Mike first got the idea that he wanted to be a doctor.

Next came a job in the circulation department of the Mt. Vernon Daily Argus. When Mr. Wendt hired me, he held up a batch of over 250 applications, from which he had interviewed many, but had chosen me. I must not have disappointed him, because years later I would run into him on the street, and he would always stop and get an update on how I was doing. The job itself was just a file clerk. Before computers, every subscriber was listed on a form, and the forms were color-coded to reflect whether that subscriber was active, inactive, on vacation, etc., and were assembled by route in small loose-leaf books. All these books were then stored in a large walk-in closet, and this was my world. I would take all incoming forms, distribute the copies to the different circulation managers, and then update the originals into the route books. Also, after the newspapers came off the press and down the chute, I would count and assign the different routes. I must have done OK here also, because no circulation manager ever yelled at me for making a mistake, either with the count or with the route books. However, it was a boring job, and too confined.

Next summer came a fun job. I don't remember how I got the word, but I went to the New York Athletic Club in Pelham (Westchester County), and got a job as a busboy. The club is a private club for the well to do, with a golf course, tennis courts, softball fields, etc., and a club-house with a magnificent restaurant and bar overlooking Long Island Sound. It had a dock, where members could come by boat or yacht. I saw a member dock a magnificent Chinese junk.

I liked the job very much. Report for work about 4PM, set up the tables for an hour or so, and then go to the kitchen to eat. The chef prepared food for the help, and it was delicious. Different from what we ate at home. We could eat as much as we wanted, but boy did he get mad if anything was left on the plate! I was also exposed to people with lots of money for the first time, and it was like peeking into another world, especially the yachts on Long Island Sound. After eating, while waiting for the restaurant to open for business, I would contemplate that world, either on the playing fields or on the water, and dreamed about being in it. I thought I looked sharp in my uniform; white shirt with black bow tie over dark pants, and a starched white jacket.

My parents were also surprised by my accomplishment, which led to an embarrassing moment. At home, I kept bragging about how beautiful the N.Y.A.C. was, so they decided to see for themselves. One night, I was called to the front desk. When I got there, I was told someone wanted to see me outside. Thoroughly puzzled, I went out, and found my mother, father, Mike, uncle Larry, and aunt Clara standing in the circular driveway entrance to the restaurant. They had taken the bus to come visit me at work. Talk about two different worlds! I asked them how they had gotten past the gate, and they said they had told the gatekeeper that they were coming to visit me. They were so obviously proud of me, which more than made up for the snickering that I'm sure was going on behind my back.

I was amazed at the tips! A guy didn't want to wait for the waiter, so he sent me to the bar to get him a drink, and he tipped me three dollars! Another time I was serving a group that had a couple of pretty girls my age at the table. They smiled at me, I smiled at them, and I made sure their water glasses were always filled. I also kept bringing fresh slabs of butter for their rolls. We were only supposed to give one slab per diner, but I just wanted to hang around that table, and look at the girls. After they left, the headwaiter told me there was a message for me at the main desk. I was given an envelope with a ten-dollar bill inside it, a tip from that dinner group. We normally didn't get tipped directly, but got a portion of the waiter's tips, about 15%. Since this was voluntary, and we didn't know how much the waiters had been tipped, there was room for larceny. Some waiters were more generous than others, and some actually tried to stiff the busboys. Fortunately, when we felt we had been short-changed, we would tell the other waiters, and they would make sure the guy recounted his tips. Mr. Rossi was the headwaiter and the person that hired me. He didn't look kindly on waiters that short-changed busboys, and that waiter might be told not to come back the next night.

Mr. Rossi also didn't care for busboys that weren't hard workers, and he liked me. So, I asked him if he wanted more people like me, and brought in a couple of guys from the neighborhood. Joey Amato was one, but I'm not sure of the others. Unfortunately, I was better when alone. I didn't take the work as seriously, and within a few weeks we were all let go. The following summer I went back by myself, and Mr. Rossi hired me again. However, the place had lost its charm, and after a month I quit. It was a great experience.

Not far from the N.Y.A.C. was Glenn Island Beach and Pool, which also had tree-shaded picnic grounds. This was our beach, even though we had to take a couple of buses to get there. My mother would prepare baskets of food and we'd leave early in the morning. Sometimes aunt Clara would come along, my father and uncle Larry on weekends. When I got older, and preferred to play ball, my mother still went with Mike. We would settle at a picnic table, and then go in the water, which wasn't far away, or pay to go into the adjoining swimming pool. Sometimes, one of the other groups had an accordion player with them, and they would of course be Italian, and play old Italian songs. I loved being tired from playing, with a belly full of my mother's cooking, laying on a blanket listening to them play and sing.

You would think that as I got older, I would wise up and not do stupid things. If you did, you would be wrong. I never really shook off 153rd Street completely. There was always the temptation to do bad things. Like the time we took a long rope, and tied one end to the wooden newsstand outside Mr. Black's candy store on White Plains Rd. We tied the other end to the back of a trolley that stopped to pick up passengers, and then watched from a hiding place while the trolley left and pulled the stand, hippety-hoppeting behind it. Fortunately, the rope broke after about a block, and the newsstand stayed intact. Still, we thought it was funny to see Mr. Black and his two kids drag the newsstand back to the store.

When Mr. Black's oldest son took over, he closed the original candy store, and built a much larger one on property that he bought on the corner of 243rd Street. He put in a jukebox, and we started to hang out there. We began to think of it as our own new clubhouse, and didn't appreciate it when people came in settled in the booths. So, we started feeding coins into the jukebox, playing the same record over and over again (The Saber Dance), and timed to see how long it would take to drive the people out. After a few times, we were the ones driven out, and told not to come back.

Our movie of choice was the RKO in Mt. Vernon. We used to go and sit in the balcony. One time, we decided to explore, and continued up the ramp to the roof. We went out on the roof, and saw that the fire escape ladder came from the street all the way to the roof. We left the roof door unlocked, and the next time we went to the movies, we went up the fire escape on the side street, up to the roof, and in by way of the unlocked door. We were very proud of ourselves, and me above all, since it had been my idea. We did this a number of times, and must have gotten careless. Someone must have seen us go up the ladder, and alerted the manager. So, after we had come in through the unlocked roof door, we walked down the ramp to the balcony level, and suddenly found ourselves surrounded by all the movie ushers, and the movie manager. We were escorted down to his office, and he was going to call the police, when he noticed my Cardinal Hayes senior ring. He asked me how I could take part in such behavior, which gave me an opportunity to do some very fast talking. I don't remember what I said, other than that we promised not to ever do it again, and he let us go.

There were other incidents, and I mention them only to show that when I say I was not a good kid, I mean I was not a good kid. Sure, I could have been worse, but I could have been so much better.

Eighteen was the legal drinking age, and a few months before that date, we started hanging out at Barney's Tavern, drinking draft beer and watching television. Television was brand new, and many homes didn't have it yet, including ours. People would stand on the sidewalk by storefronts to watch it. Because Barney's sponsored "The Scarlets" baseball team, which was made up of guys a couple of years older than us, we were OK. Actually, Roddy had been asked to play on their team, and then I was also invited to join. So, we would gather at Barney's, listen to adult jokes from the older guys, and watch Antonino Rocco wrestle on TV. He was a marvel, and as soon as we got a TV, my father became a wrestling nut. He would sit in front of that TV, twisting and turning with his hero of the evening, and especially Antonino. Fortunately, Antonino almost never lost, because my father would curse for days about how his hero had been "robbed". My father remained a wrestling fanatic to the day he died, and he never believed for a second that any of those matches were "fixed".

Speaking of "The Scarlets" and my father brings to mind a story. The older guys asked me to play on their team for a basketball game they had. Anxious to look gook, I played a very aggressive game, maybe too aggressive. That was the reason I was all by myself, on the opposite side of the court, trying to steal the ball, when I committed a flagrant foul. The guy wasn't going to take that from a pipsqueak like me, so he dropped the ball, and gave me a big shove. I immediately answered with a big punch, and the next second the one guy became ten. I actually counted about a hundred before the lights went out. The team came to my rescue, and removed me from the bottom of the pile. I was done for the game, had no broken bones, but the makings of a beautiful shiner (black eye). After the game, we went Barney's for a beer, and I was one of the guys. I was trying to figure a good way to explain the black eye to my folks, when I made a bad situation much worse. My nose was running, so I took a handkerchief and blew it. The pressure forced blood into my eyelid, making it swell like a balloon, and shutting it tight.

I had no options. I waited outside the house until I saw the light go on in the bedroom, which meant my father was going to bed because he had to go to work the next day. Then I went upstairs, and threw myself at my mother's mercy. She understood the situation, and agreed to cover for me. My father would have gotten needlessly upset, and he already didn't approve of my ball playing. I would have gotten away with it, if my father had not come through my bedroom in the morning, on the way to check the outside temperature. He saw my eye, became very alarmed, and called my mother. I heard everything, but made believe I was still sleeping. When my mother came, she gave an Oscar-winning performance. She told my father that she was as surprised as he was, especially since she had seen me when I had come home, and I was OK. Then she came up with the solution. She pointed out that the bedroom windows were partially open, and it had been a very cold night. I must have caught a cold in the eye. My father wasn't buying the story, so I "woke up" from the noise, and was alarmed that I couldn't open my eye. My mother came over to reassure me everything would be all right. What could my father do? He walked away shaking his head, and my mother gave me a look of exasperation that said she had almost had it with me. Almost, but never quite! God bless her.

Regis Philbin and I graduate from Cardinal Hayes

Well, I graduated from Cardinal Hayes in June of '49 with an above B average. The ceremony was at St. Patrick's Cathedral in Manhattan, after which we went home, and had a family celebration with uncle Larry and aunt Clara. I had taken an entrance exam to NYU, had been accepted, and was supposed to start classes in September. Somewhere along the way, I had decided I wanted to be a mechanical engineer (I suppose because my best subject was math), and NYU was a very good school.

For my fifteen minutes of fame, I should mention that Regis Philbin and I shared to same homeroom in our senior year. Although we didn't hang out together, we signed each other's yearbook, and he was fascinated with the pronunciation of my last name. He took a particular delight in yelling it out loud every time he saw me in the hallways, in that staccato manner that became his trademark and that he carries to this day, (Scian-ca-le-<u>po</u>-re) with the accent on the "po".

Many years later, I attended a class reunion that Regis hosted, with George Carlin as guest ex-Hayes man, and brought my wife and children. During a break, I saw Regis was alone at the buffet table, and figured it was a good time to go over and say hello. Many years had passed, and my name had changed, but as he saw me approach, he pointed his forefinger at me, and yelled, "Scian-ca-le-<u>po</u>-re!" Then, he just walked away with his food! Apparently, we still weren't buddies!

A change in plans

Sometime during the summer I came up with a better plan. I really wanted to be a professional baseball player, and I wanted to give that a shot first, while I was at the right age. I convinced my parents. Actually, I convinced my mother, and my father went along with it, so long as it wouldn't cost him any money. I proceeded to enroll for a tryout camp run by the Washington Senators. It was for a month, and was to start the first week of January '50.
This gave me time to get a job and put some money away. How I got the job is a good story.

We used to play softball on an empty lot on 242nd Street. Occasionally, we would play baseball, and the lot was too small for that. So, it happened that I hit a baseball too far, and it went across the next street, and broke a window. Instead of running away, I went to the house, apologized, and offered to replace the windowpane. I took the measurements, went to the hardware store, got the glass and the putty, and replaced the pane. The elderly couple was appreciative, and apparently never forgot it.

The summer after graduation, my father was doing some brickwork on their house, and told them of my plans. Well, they called their son, who was a judge working in the city, and he got me a job immediately. It was in lower Manhattan, near the waterfront, with the Cudahy Meat Company. I worked the night shift, unloading the freight cars that were parked on the tracks upstairs, and loading the trucks parked on the loading bay downstairs. It was manly work, and I was the only kid there. The winter nights were cold, and we moved frozen meats from freight cars to refrigerator, or from refrigerator to refrigerated trucks. Boy, did we look forward to those coffee breaks! I became friendly with a young fellow in his middle twenty's, and another older man. They both lived uptown, although not as far as me, and we would sometimes stop off on the way home to get an early breakfast together. When I came back from Florida, I went to visit the younger fellow, and only then found out that he was actually an undercover agent hired by the company. It seems there had been a pretty significant ring that had been stealing from Cudahy, including foremen, truck drivers, and salesmen. It was pretty neat. They had no overhead. Their salesmen would sell the merchandise, they would then steal it from Cudahy, and deliver it with Cudahy's trucks. They specialized in prized meats in small packages, which made it easier to sneak it past the personnel not involved in the thievery. I was told that after I had left, there had been quite a few arrests.

Some nights, especially the colder ones, I didn't feel like going to work, so I would play "hooky". I couldn't stay home, because I had no good reason not to go to work, especially since it was only for a short time, and I needed every dollar I could earn. So, I would spend some hours at Barney's, drinking beer and watching TV. After the bar closed at 3 AM, I would drive around for a couple of hours, and then go home. Actually, it was a pretty boring way to spend the night, but I liked working even less. I really only did it a couple of times, and I'll tell you why I didn't do it any more. Once, as I was driving around in the middle of the night, I drove through a red light. There was no one on the streets, so I just ignored the signal. Actually, there must have been someone around, because a police car materialized out of nowhere, and pulled me over. They checked me and searched the car thoroughly. They found nothing, and I told them the truth. They decided to give me a break, and not give me a ticket, on condition that I would go straight home. I agreed. However, on the way home, the little devil that always gives me bad advice, did it again. I wondered why I should go home when I didn't want to, especially since the cops were gone, and the streets were deserted. I decided to challenge authority again, but I took no chances. I swerved into a side street, and proceeded with lefts and rights, so as to lose anyone that may have been following me. I was very proud of my driving, and after about a half hour of maneuvering on the back streets, I emerged on a main road. Imagine my surprise when I found that same police car waiting for me there! They didn't bother to talk to me. Just signaled me to follow them to the 49th Precinct Police Station. There, they had me empty my pockets, and were going to put me in jail. But just as I have a devil on one shoulder, I have an angel on the other one. A big cop named "Guilly" passed by, and he knew me. He lived across the street from me, and his daughter had a crush on Richie. Guilly vouched for me, and I showed them my Cardinal Hayes school ring. Once again, Cardinal Hayes High School's reputation saved my skin. The cops told me to go home, and that they would check my house in 30 minutes. If my car wasn't there, I would be in really big trouble! Boy, did I show them! I was home and in bed in less than fifteen minutes!

Now I was ready for the next big jump of my life! Leaving home for the first time, with the heady possibility that I was taking the first step towards a life as a Major League baseball player, possibly with the Yankees. Why not? If I was going to dream, I was going to dream big! Imagine, me playing center field after Joe DiMaggio retired! I was very excited, and couldn't wait to get started.

Somewhere in my mind was an awareness that my kid days were over, and I should be more serious about planning my future. I had no trouble making sure that those thoughts didn't surface. I wasn't ready to grow up.

*   *   *

EPILOGUE

This closes my decade of the forties, and so many first experiences. There are so many more, that either didn't come to mind, or I just felt weren't significant enough to include. Otherwise, it might take me ten years to write about those ten years

Even as I write, some come to mind. I remember my cat "Boots" walking with me down the street every morning when I left for school. He would sit at the corner until I was out of sight, and then go back home. Mike tells me he did the same thing when the family went out, and took the trolley.

I remember getting sick with bronchitis every winter, and my mother babying me with soup and toast, alcohol rubdowns, and buying me comic books. This was also the first time I cried reading a book. I was fourteen, and it was Dickens' "Oliver Twist". These were also occasions when Dr. Cerrato and I would tease each other, since his son attended Mount St. Michael, archrival of Cardinal Hayes. Worse yet, he was the doctor for their football team, and was on the field when their team beat ours more often than not on our traditional Thanksgiving Day game. I always accused him of prescribing those terrible sulfur pills on purpose.

I remember going to the YMCA in Mt Vernon to play basketball, and to swim in the pool in the wintertime.

I remember my imaginary friends, "Scoop" Daily and "Ham". I don't know where I got "Scoop" from, but "Ham" was a bodyguard for "Mandrake the Magician" from the comics, I think. Big muscular guy with curly black hair, but not too bright. "Scoop" had the brains. Anyway, whenever I would be walking home alone at night from the movies, they would go ahead of me and check out the neighborhood to make sure it was safe for me to go ahead. Then one or the other would report back, and we'd talk to each other out loud. They were great guys and totally devoted to me.

*　　*　　*